THE REAL MESSIAH?

*A Jewish Response
to Missionaries*

ARYEH KAPLAN

Published by OU/NCSY Publications,
Orthodox Union, Eleven Broadway, New York, NY 10004.
212.563.4000 • info@ou.org • www.ou.org.

Distributed by Mesorah Publications, Inc., 4401 Second Avenue,
Brooklyn, NY 11232. Distributed in Israel by Sifriati/A. Gitler
Books, 6 Hayarkon Street, Bnai Brak 51127. Distributed in Europe
by Lehmanns, Unit E, Viking Industrial Park, Rolling Mill Road,
Jarow, NE32 3DP, England. Distributed in Australia and New Zealand by
Golds World of Judaica, 3-13 William Street, Balaclava, Melbourne 3183
Victoria, Australia. Distributed in South Africa by Kollel Bookshop, Shop
8A, Norwood Hypermarket, Norwood 2196, Johannesburg, South Africa.

ISBN 1-879016-11-7

PRINTED IN THE UNITED STATES OF AMERICA

In memory of my dear parents

אפרים פישל בן דב בער, ז"ל

and

אלטא מירל בת ברוך דוד, ז"ל

ת׳נ׳צ׳ב׳ה׳

This publication has been
made possible through

The
FISCHEL AND ALTA TENNENBAUM
Memorial Foundation קרן פישל ואלטא טעננבוים ע"ה

CONTENTS

Very often, in an attempt to respond to a missionary challenge, one can make a number of seemingly logical moves which, in fact, play directly into the hands of the missionaries. Therefore, a number of Jewish communal leaders have prepared these guidelines for dealing on the spot with missionaries and their followers.

A PRACTICAL GUIDE TO THE MISSIONARY PROBLEM

1) You will not win hearts to Torah by trying to convince people that the claims of Christianity are false. Spend your time learning, teaching and explaining the meaning of the Torah and its Mitsvos. Better still, invite a person who is in search of religious values to a Shabbaton, or to your home for Shabbat. Let the truth and beauty of Torah and its way of life restore people to the right path.

2) Do not argue with missionaries; do not lend credence or dignity to their efforts at soul snatching. There are tens of millions of non-practicing Christians in this country who are better targets for their efforts.

3) Missionaries are usually closed-minded fanatics. They are trained to respond to your arguments with pat, almost memorized answers. If they can't handle your objection, they will deflect it by raising another, and still another point. Even if you win—you lose.

4) Do not debate, dialogue or argue with missionaries. Missionaries often seek to engage Jews in public discussion. Do not be drawn into this utterly fruitless exercise. Above all, do not invite missionaries or their followers to address meetings under Jewish auspices. Such hospitality only gives the missionary cause institutional dignity and legitimacy. On the other hand, do not publicly attack or abuse the missionaries; this merely serves to surround them with an aura of martyrdom, to our loss. Our essential obligation is to shore up our Jewishness.

5) Do not be taken in by the "Jewish Christian" ploy. Some missionary groups appeal specifically to Jews with the specious notion that those joining them are thereby "completed" or "fulfilled" as Jews. This is patently incompatible with Jewish tradition and conviction. Conversion to Christianity or any other faith is an abandonment of Judaism. We must strive, with loving concern, to restore erring individuals to their own faith and community.

6) Do not lose your "cool." The style of the missionaries is likely to be cool and affable. Emulate it. When they come smiling to the door, respond politely—firmly but with no recrimination—"No, thanks, I'm not interested," or some brief and definitive equivalent.

7) Get the facts. Fact-finding is a "must." This is an indispensable step. Until the actual situation in the community has been established, planning cannot proceed intelligently. Are Jews, as Jews, being missionized? By whom, from what centers or sources? In what settings and by what means—in schools, through coffee houses, "drop-in" centers, via the communications media, prayer meetings, home study groups, bookmobiles?

8) Plan strategy and approaches. Assuming the fact-gathering process indicates a problem requiring action:

(a) Survey the available resources—knowledgeable and experienced personnel, appropriate literature, suitable facilities.

(b) Priority should go to marshalling individuals—young and old. Set up a task force of peer-to-peer as well as adult resource people with some forte or expertise in this area.

(c) *Very carefully* study *at first hand* the needs of those Jewish young people who are flirting with or have been drawn into other religious movements, and what they are seeking. *Make no prejudgments* on these matters. The Jesus Movement is very complex.

(d) With equal care plan how to offer a positive Jewish response to their need and search. Only then will it be possible to reach out to them and to share the needed knowledge and understanding with others to be trained for further intensive outreach.

9) Focus on the teenager. Not only college students, but those in the high schools and even in the junior high schools must be deemed vulnerable. Many missionaries may concentrate on teenagers, deliberately using a peer-group approach, exploiting the unsettled state that marks the adolescent years particularly in these times, and the readiness of young people to challenge any traditional accepted values. These areas demand our greatest scrutiny and innovative planning. Our caution against overreaction bears repeating

here. "Crash programs," counter-crusades, or resort to gimmickry must be avoided.

10) Create opportunities for youth participation. Unfortunately those who are confused Jewishly and troubled personally will not always avail themselves of the programs conducted in synagogues, or youth organizations. Additional ways need to be developed for reaching out with approaches that truly enable young people to shape the content, directions and policies of the programs in which they participate, including those programs that *are regarded by them* as not controlled by the "establishment." Some recently initiated youth and teen programs reflect this approach, utilizing informal settings such as storefronts and coffee houses, providing opportunity for "rapping" and for making contacts with other youth. Such programs are consistent with the long range goals of reaching youth, providing a Jewish setting in which they can relax, meet other Jewish youth, "shmoos" and talk seriously with warm, sensitive, responsive and skillful people—including members of their own peer-groups. Experimentation with innovative and creative approaches to opening channels of participation by our youth must be given high priority.

Most of all, remember that most people drawn to the missionaries have never experienced real Torah living—just suggest "before you go to the gentiles, why not see what our own tradition has to offer." But follow through by making positive Torah experiences available to them.

For almost 2,000 years, Christian missionaries have been trying to convince the Jew to accept their beliefs, and for just as long, the Jew has resisted. The ones who resisted most strongly were those who sought G-d with the most fervor. What was their motivation? Why did we never give in to the missionaries?

WHY AREN'T WE CHRISTIANS?

by

ARYEH KAPLAN

We hear quite a bit today about a movement called "Jews for Jesus." A small number of Jews seem to be finding the teachings of Christianity very attractive. The vast majority of Jews, however, still reject these teachings in the most emphatic terms.

For almost two thousand years, the Christians have been trying to win over the Jew. And for the same period of time, the Jew has resisted all such overtures. But why? Why don't we accept Jesus? In short: Why aren't we Christians?

In order to understand this, we must look at the origin of Christian beliefs. Christianity began with a Jew. Jesus lived as a Jew, around the same time as many of our greatest Talmudic sages. The great Hillel lived just a generation earlier, and Rabbi Akiba, a generation after. Our own sources, however, record very little about Jesus' life. Every-

thing that we know about him is found in the Gospels of
the New Testament, a book written by and for the early
Christian church. This book, however, was written primarily to further the cause of Christianity, and it is therefore
impossible to separate the historical person of Jesus from
the "Christ" required by early Christian theology.

Soon after the death of Jesus, we find a marked change
in the teachings of his followers. Christianity as we know it
began during this period in the work of Paul of Tarsus.
Paul, or as he was earlier known, Saul, was a disciple of the
great Talmudist Rabbi Gamliel, and he began his career by
actively opposing the early Christians. In a dramatic incident on the road to Damascus, Paul converted to Christianity, and later became one of its foremost leaders. Although
he had never seen Jesus alive, he claimed to have spoken to
him in spirit. Under Paul's leadership, many of the distinc-
tive doctrines of Christianity were first proclaimed, and, for
the most part, they have never changed. His teachings are
recorded in his Epistles, which form the second part of the
New Testament.

Among Paul's major teachings, we find the following:

1. Jesus was the Messiah or Christ predicted by the
   Prophets of the Bible and awaited by the Jews. He
   is also the Son of G-d, and like any son, is essentially
   the same as his Father.

2. Man is evil and sinful. All mankind is damned because of Adam's sin. The Torah cannot save man,
   since its many commandments make it too difficult
   to keep. The only thing that can prevent man's utter
   damnation in hell is the belief in Christ.

3. The Jews were originally G-d's chosen people, but they were rejected when they refused to accept His son, Jesus. The name "Israel," G-d's chosen people, is no longer carried by the Jew, but by those who accept Jesus as the Messiah. Only these share G-d's love. Everyone else is damned in hell.

4. There is only one law now that Christ has come, and that is love. One must follow the example of Christ's sacrifice, and patiently hope that G-d will be gracious in return.

It is enough to state these articles of Christian faith to see why the Jews could not accept them. Taking them one by one, the Jewish viewpoint would be:

1. Jesus could not have been the Messiah. The Prophets predicted a world of peace and love after the Messiah's coming, and this certainly does not exist today. Furthermore, any talk of the Messiah as being the "son of G-d" is totally unacceptable. In no place do the Prophets say that he will be anything more than a remarkable leader and teacher.

2. Although the Torah does speak of Adam's sin, it teaches that man can rise above it. Man might not be able to perfect himself, but it was for this reason that G-d gave us the Torah. It is absurd to think that G-d would give a Torah that was impossible or too difficult to follow. In no place does Judaism teach that one can be saved from damnation by mere belief. Any true belief in G-d must lead a person to also follow His commandments.

3. It is impossible to imagine that G-d would ever reject the Jewish people. In many places, the Bible clearly states that His covenant with them will be forever.

4. In many places, the Bible says that the Torah was given forever. It is therefore impossible to say that it has been replaced by a new law or testament. Love alone is not enough, for one must know how to express it, and for this, we need the Torah as a guide. Love is only one of the Torah's commandments, and good deeds are its necessary expression.

Why do we believe these ideas rather than the ones expressed by Paul and Christianity?

For one thing, we see no evidence that Jesus was indeed the Messiah expected by Israel. The Messianic promise included such things as perfect peace and unity among men, love and truth, universal knowledge and undisturbed happiness, as well as the end of all evil, idolatry, falsehood and hatred. None of these things have been fulfilled by Christianity.

The Christian answer to this is the simple assertion that all things have indeed changed by the coming of Jesus. If the change is not visible, it is because man is evil and has not truly accepted Jesus and his teachings. Thus, the Messiah or Christ will have to return in order to prove his victory.

The Jew refuses to accept the excuse that the major prophecies concerning the Messiah will only be fulfilled in a "second coming." He expects the Messiah to complete his mission in his first attempt. The Jew therefore believes that the Messiah is yet to come.

But there is also another more important issue at stake than the mere identity of the Messiah. Christianity teaches that Jesus was also G-d in human form. The Jew sees this as a totally mistaken idea about G-d. It makes G-d too small, for in stating that He can assume human form, it diminishes both His unity and His divinity.

We disagree with Christianity not only with regard to belief, but also with regard to what man must do. Christianity tends to deny that man's actions are ultimately very useful. The only thing that can save man is his utter despair in his own sinfulness, and total dependence on G-d. The Jew, on the other hand, believes that man can come close to G-d by obeying Him and keeping His commandments.

Christianity thus starts with one idea about man, while Judaism starts with the exact opposite idea.

Judaism starts with the idea that man is created in the "likeness of G-d." He therefore does not have to go very far to discover the divine, both in himself and in others. There is always the opportunity to awaken the divine in oneself by obeying G-d's commandments. The Jew begins with this opportunity.

Christianity, on the other hand, begins with the basic assumption that man is depraved and sinful. Left to himself, man is utterly damned. He is naturally involved in evil, and must therefore do something to be saved from it.

The first question that the Christian asks is, "What have you done to be saved?" To the Jew, this question is almost meaningless. This is not the Jewish way of thinking at all. The Jew asks, "How can I serve G-d? How can I keep His commandments?" The central focus of Judaism is obeying the commandments of the Torah. We look at man and see his greatness, for he can obey these commandments and fulfill G-d's will.

Christianity teaches that man is so evil that he can never really serve G-d. The Torah is too difficult for man. The only thing that man can do is believe in Christ and wait for salvation.

The Jew replies that the very fact that G-d Himself gave us commandments and told us to obey them teaches us that we can indeed serve G-d and fulfill His will. It is unthinkable that G-d would give His people a Torah if it were impossible to keep it.

Although all of Jesus' disciples were Jews, they could not convince their fellow Jews of their teachings. The early dogmas of Christianity seemed closer to those of the pagan gentiles than to those of the Jews. More and more, Christianity was rejected by the Jews and accepted by the gentiles. It thus gradually developed into a gentile church, and its attitude toward the Jews became more and more unfriendly. It may have constantly appealed to the Jews to convert, sometimes even resorting to cruelty and force, but the Jew stood firm. Christianity may have changed human history, but it could never win over the Jews. The Jew stood by his Torah and walked his own way.

In essence, there were two Christian teachings that the Jew could never accept. Christianity taught that G-d had assumed human form in Jesus, and that the Torah no longer mattered. The Jew rejected these two dogmas, even under pain of death.

In rejecting Christianity, Judaism therefore did not reject anything that it needed spiritually. There was nothing in all the teachings of Jesus that would have added even one iota to the strength of the Torah. If Christianity made any contribution at all, it was to the non-Jewish world.

The Jew knew that his Torah provided him with a unique relationship with G-d. Everything that he saw in Christianity seemed to contradict this relationship. It is for this reason that throughout the centuries, the Jew has found it impossible to accept the teachings of Christianity. He believed with perfect faith that G-d had shown him the way, and he had no intention of ever leaving it.

For the Jew, accepting Christianity involved much more than merely accepting a false Messiah. Aside from its belief in Jesus as the Messiah, Christianity has altered many of the most fundamental concepts of Judaism. Here, we explore the Halachic consequences of a Jew who embraces Christianity.

WHEN A JEW BECOMES A CHRISTIAN

by

ARYEH KAPLAN

The sign shouts, "Jews for Jesus!"

You look at the sign and wonder what's going on. You might have heard of them or read about them in the papers. Your curiosity is aroused.

You decide to find out more about it, and speak to one of these strange people. You strike up a conversation. He tells you that he is a Jewish Christian,—one of the "Jews for Jesus."

Before you know it, he is asking you how you feel about your Jewishness. You might admit that you find your Judaism spiritually unfulfilling. You both agree that the typical liberal synagogue in which you grew up seemed to offer everything but a religious experience.

You admit that deep down you realize that there is a spiritual dimension missing from your life. He sympathizes and tells you the reason why Judaism does not fulfill this need is because you have left out an essential ingredient.

Then he gives you the punch line: What you need is Jesus. He tells you that to be a true Jew you must believe in Jesus. Only then, so he says, can Judaism provide you with that dimension you are seeking.

Do not be deceived.

For the past two thousand years, Christians have been trying to convert Jews to their beliefs. This is a central goal of their religion. Jesus, the central object of their belief, was a Jew. He taught and preached to Jews. Yet, he was rejected by them. How can Christians justify their belief, when Jesus' very own people refused to accept him? To get the Jews to accept Jesus is therefore one of their most important goals. However, in our generation, some enlightened Christian leaders have called for an end to such active missionary activity. Sadly enough, these leaders are ignored by the growing missionary "cult."

But you might ask, "So what's that terrible? At worst I'll be believing in a false Messiah. What do I have to lose?"

The truth is that you have a lot to lose.

Let us begin by examining the basic beliefs of Christianity.

Beside its basic creed that Jesus was the Messiah, the fundamental doctrines of Christianity are:

The Trinity: According to most Christians, G-d consists of three persons, the Father, the Son, and the Holy Ghost.

The Incarnation: Christians believe that the Son, the second part of the godhead, came down to earth in human form in the person of Jesus.

Mediation: According to their creed, no man can approach G-d directly. Everyone must go through Jesus, the Son.

Let us carefully examine these beliefs.

A basic foundation of most Christian sects is belief in the Trinity. Christianity teaches that G-d consists of three persons, the Father, the Son, and the Holy Ghost. The Father is the one who created the world, the Son is the one who redeems man, and the Holy Ghost is the member of the godhead that speaks to the prophets.[1]

Jesus himself alluded to the doctrine of the Trinity. The Gospel of Matthew tells us that his final words to his disciples was, "Go ye therefore, and teach all nations, baptizing them in the name of the Father, and of the Son, and of the Holy Ghost."[2] This belief in a three-part god is a basic doctrine of Christianity.

Christians claim that this three-part god that they worship is the same as the G-d worshipped by the Jews.

This is not true.

The Bible states (Deut. 6:4), "Hear O Israel, the L-rd is our G-d, the L-rd is *One*."

Twice every day, the believing Jew cries out these words. They are the first thing a Jew learns as a child and the last words he utters before he dies. On every Jewish doorpost there is a Mezuzah proclaiming these words. They are again found in the Tefillin, bound daily next to a Jew's heart and mind, proclaiming this most basic principle of Judaism.

Worship of any three-part god by a Jew is nothing less than a form of idolatry.[3]

Idolatry does not necessarily mean worshipping a god of stone or wood. Even if a Jew worships the highest angel, it is also a form of idolatry.[4] G-d is the infinite One, Creator of all things. Anyone who worships anything else is guilty of idolatry.[5]

The three-part God of Christianity is not the G-d of Judaism. Therefore, in the Jewish view, Christianity may very well be a variation of idolatry.

Although Christianity began among Jews, it was rapidly adopted by the pagans of the ancient world. These pagans believed in an entire pantheon of gods. It was just too much for them to give up all these gods in favor of the One True G-d. So early Christian missionaries compromised with these pagans by introducing the Trinity, a sort of three-in-one god. Even many contemporary Christian scholars see the Trinity as the result of pagan influence on Christianity.

This might represent an improvement for the pagan. But for the Jew it is a regression, representing a step backwards towards idolatry.

This might not seem to be in the Jewish spirit of never attacking other faiths, but when missionaries are spreading lies about Judaism, it is time to unmask these lies. Indeed, several contemporary Christian leaders have denounced the missionaries who prey on Jews.

Let us now examine a second basic belief of Christianity, that of the Incarnation. According to this doctrine, G-d in the person of the Son assumed human form in the person of Jesus.

It is best expressed in the Nicene Creed, recited every Sunday in most churches. In it, the Christian declares:

"I believe in one Lord, Jesus Christ, the only-begotten Son of God. Born of the Father before all ages. God of God, Light of Light, true God of true God. Begotten, not made, of one substance with the Father. By whom all things were made. Who for us men and for our salvation came down from heaven. And he became flesh by the Holy Spirit of the Virgin Mary: and was made man."

Christians really believe that Jesus was G-d, and this is one of the most fundamental beliefs of Christianity.

If we accept the testimony of the Gospels, then this belief originated with Jesus himself.

Among other things, Jesus said:

"All things that the Father (i.e. G-d) hath are mine."[6]

"My father worketh hitherto, and I work."[7]

"For the Father judgeth no man, but hath committed all judgement unto the Son; that all men should honour the Son, even as they honour the Father."[8]

"I and the Father are one."[9]

"He that hath seen me hath seen the Father."[10]

From these quotes, it seems obvious that Jesus himself claimed to be G-d. The missionaries and "Jews for Jesus" do not tell you about this. They wait until you have fallen into their net. But this is one of the most basic beliefs of Christianity.

If belief in the Trinity is idolatry, then, from the Jewish point of view, this concept is perhaps even more objectionable. The pagan gods came down in human form, copulated with mortals, and bore human children. Many Christian historians attribute it to the early Christians who were attempting to win over pagans to their new religion, and therefore adopted this pagan concept.

But what does the Bible say about the unity of G-d?

It says:

"Know this day, and lay it in your heart, that the L-rd is G-d, in the heavens above and on the earth below, there is none else." (Deut. 4:39)

"Do I not fill heaven and earth, says G-d." (Jer. 25:24)

"The whole earth is filled with his glory." (Isa. 6:3)

"Great is G-d, highly praised, His greatness is un-fathomable." (Psalms 145:3)

G-d is the Ultimate, the Infinite, the All Powerful Creator of all things. To say that any man was G-d is, to the Jew, the height of absurdity.

The Bible says (Numbers 23:19), "G-d is not a mortal that He should lie, nor a man, that He should change His mind." G-d does not suddenly decide to visit the earth in a human body. A G-d who fills and sustains all creation does not have to visit our planet in human form. The Jerusalem Talmud flatly states the Jewish view, "If a man claims to be G-d, he is a liar!"[11]

The third basic belief of Christianity is that of Mediation. This states that man cannot approach G-d except through Jesus. All prayer must be in the name of "Jesus Christ our Lord."

Here again, it was Jesus himself who is alleged to have proclaimed this doctrine. He openly said, "I am the way, the truth, and the life, no man cometh unto the Father but by me."[12]

This Christian doctrine goes against the very opening statement of the Ten Commandments.

The Ten Commandments begin with the words, "I am the L-rd your G-d, Who brought you out of the Land of Egypt, from the house of slavery. You shall have no other gods *before Me.*"

When G-d says "Before Me," He is stressing that you should not believe in any other deity, even if You believe in G-d as well. One who sets up a mediator between G-d and man is guilty of violating this Commandment.[13]

If a man believes in G-d, then why should he need any other deity? But a person might think that G-d is so high as to be unapproachable without a mediator. The opening statement of the Ten Commandments teaches us that this is also idolatry.

G-d is infinite and all-knowing. To say that He needs a mediator to hear our prayers is to deny His infinite wisdom.

If Jesus actually made these statements recorded in the Gospel, then he was advocating idolatry, with himself as the deity. If this is true, is there any wonder that Jews never accepted him either as prophet, rabbi or teacher?

Judaism is unique among the religions of the world. Almost without exception, the world's religions begin with a single individual, be he Jesus, or Buddah, or Mohammed, or Confucius, or Lao-tze. This individual gradually gathers a following, either through "miracles" or through sheer charisma. But from the beginning the entire foundation rests on a single individual.

Judaism is the one exception to this. It did not begin with any individual. An entire nation stood at the foot of Mount Sinai and heard G-d introduce Himself.

Only G-d, speaking to an entire nation could reveal a true religion. And once G-d speaks, He does not "change His mind," or revise the truths He proclaimed as absolute and eternal.

Our most basic beliefs were taught by G-d Himself at Sinai. The Bible says (Deut. 4:35), "Unto you it was shown, that you might know, that the L-rd is G-d, there is none else besides Him. Out of heaven He made you hear His voice, that He might instruct you."

No matter how many miracles a prophet might produce, he cannot change this basic principle. If a man tells us to commit idolatry, he is a false prophet, no matter how many wonders he pulls out of a hat.

G-d warned us about this in the Bible (Deut. 13:2):

"If there arise among you a prophet, or a dreamer, and he gives you a sign or a miracle. And the sign or miracle comes to pass, and he calls on you, saying, 'Let us go after other gods, whom you have not known, and let us worship them.' You shall not listen to that prophet or dreamer. For G-d is testing you, to see whether you love the L-rd your G-d with all your heart and with all your soul."

G-d Himself was warning us about movements like Christianity. Even if all the miracles recorded in the Gospel were true, we do not pay any heed to them. G-d has already warned us.

This brings us back to our original question. What can a Jew lose by embracing Christianity?

The answer is: Everything.

Christianity negates the fundamentals of Jewish faith, and one who accepts it rejects the very essence of Judaism.[14] Even if he continues to keep all the rituals, it is the same as if he abandoned Judaism completely. The Talmud teaches us, "Whoever accepts idolatry, denies the entire Torah."[15]

A Jew who accepts Christianity might call himself a "Jewish Christian," but he is no longer a Jew.[16] He can no longer even be counted as part of a Jewish congregation.[17]

Conversion to another faith is an act of religious treason. It is one of the worst possible sins that a Jew can commit. Along with murder and incest, it is one of the three cardinal sins which may not be violated even under pain of death.[18]

The missionaries tell you, "Believe in Jesus and be saved."

The truth is that one who falls into their net is eternally cast away from before his G-d.

A Jew must give his life rather than embrace Christianity.[19]

This is not mere rhetoric. Throughout our history, millions of Jews were given this choice: The Cross or death. Invariably, they chose death.

The missionaries now come and preach love and peace. But Jesus himself said, "Think not that I come to send peace on earth. I come not to send peace, but the sword."[20]

In was this sword that the Crusaders used to wipe out hundreds of Jewish communities in the name of Jesus, the Jew.

It was this sword that they used when they entered Jerusalem in 1215. Their first act was to round up all the Jews to the central synagogue and burn them to death.

It was this sword used by the Spanish Inquisition, when they tortured Jews to death in the name of "Christian Love."

Remember all this when the "Jews for Jesus" speak of peace and love.

These "Jews for Jesus" may arouse your curiosity. But they should also arouse your pity. For they are in an inherent paradox. A Jew for Jesus is a contradiction in terms.

*   *   *

But what about the Jew who has embraced Christianity? What about the one who has already taken Jesus as his "savior."

Is he eternally cut off from Judaism? Is he lost without hope of redemption? Is he totally cut off from his people and his G-d?

Judaism teaches that there is always hope.

No matter how far one strays from G-d and Torah he is always accepted back.

The Bible says:

"As I live, says G-d, I have no pleasure in the death of the wicked, but that they turn from their way and live." (Ezek. 33:11).

"When the wicked turns from his sin, and does what is lawful and right, he shall live thereby." (*Ibid.* 33:19).

"That every man shall return from his way, and I will forgive him." (Jer. 36:3)

"If they return to You, and confess Your Name, and pray . . . then You will hear in Heaven, and forgive their sin." (1 Kings 8:33, 34)

Even a Jew who has embraced another religion is given a second chance. He can still return to Judaism and be re-accepted by G-d.

He must completely disavow Christianity for all time and commit himself totally and without reservation to

Judaism. He need not be formally "converted" back to Judaism, but a definite committment is in order.[21]

Christianity for a Jew is a form of idolatry, and must be repented as such. Our sages teach us that keeping the Sabbath is particularly effective for such atonement.[22]

*   *   *

If you find your life spiritually empty, devoid of religious experience, then you need Torah Judaism all the more. You might been been turned off by the pseudo-intellectual substitutes offered by certain "liberal" rabbis. You may never have been exposed to the true depths of Judaism. But it is there, and millions of Jews are inspired by it.

I can gaze at a beautiful sunset, and try to describe it to you. But until you open your eyes and see it for yourself, my words are in vain. You must see it to appreciate it.

I can describe the most delicious fruit. But you must taste it to appreciate it.

The same is true of Judaism. The Bible tells us (Ps. 34:9), "Taste and see, that G-d is good, happy is the man who embraces Him."

You must actually live Torah Judaism to appreciate its beauty and wisdom. Only when you immerse yourself in it totally will you discover its full spiritual dimension.

NOTES

1. Nicene Creed.
2. Matthew 28:19. All quotations are from the King James' Version.
3. *Emunos VeDeyos* 2:5–7, *Moreh Nevuchim* 1:50, Beginning of *Maamar Techiyas Ha-Mesim* (Rambam); *Tshuvos Meil Tzedakah* 22, *Tshuvos Shaar Ephraim* 24, Chasam Sofer on *Orech Chaim* 156:1.
4. *Yad, Avodas Kochavim* 2:1.
5. *Kesef Mishneh, Lechem Mishneh,* on *Yad, Tshuvah* 3:7.
6. John 16:14.
7. *Ibid.* 5:17.
8. *Ibid.* 5:22.
9. *Ibid.* 10:30.
10. *Ibid.* 14:9.
11. *Yerushalmi, Taanis* 2:1 (91). Cf. *Moreh Nevuchim* 3:15.
12. John 14:6.
13. *Yad, Avodas Kochavim* 1.
14. *Ibid., Yesodei HaTorah* 1:6.
15. *Sifri* on Num. 15:22 and Deut. 11:28; *Yad, Avodas Kochavim* 2:4. Cf. *Horios* 8a.
16. *Yad, loc. cit.* 2:5.
17. *Pri Megadim, Eshel Avraham* 55:4.
18. *Sanhedrin* 74a.
19. *Tshuvos Rivash* 4, 11, *Tshuvos Rabbi Yosef ben Lev* 1:15.
20. Matthew 10:34. Cf. Luke 12:49, 51.
21. It is recommended that such a penitent undergo the ritual of immersion like a convert. See *Nimukey Yosef, Yebamos, Rif* 16b *"Kedusnav," Yoreh Deah* 268:12 in *Hagah, Turey Zahav Ibid.* 267:5, *Magen Avraham* 325:8. Cf. *Avos DeRabbi Nathan* 8:8.
22. *Shabbos* 118b; *Tur, Orech Chaim* 242.

*To the Jew, the Messiah has a most important mission,
namely to bring the world back to G-d, and make it a place
of peace, justice and harmony. When Jesus failed to
accomplish this, the early Christians had to radically alter
the very concept of the Messiah. This, in turn, transformed
Christianity from another Jewish Messianic sect into a
religion that is quite alien to many basic Jewish teachings.*

FROM MESSIAH TO CHRIST
by
ARYEH KAPLAN

Belief in the coming of the Messiah has always been
a fundamental part of Judaism. Thus, for example,
Maimonides counts the belief in the Messiah as one of the
thirteen cardinal principles of Judaism. It is a concept that is
repeated again and again throughout the length and
breadth of Jewish literature.

There have been many people in Jewish history who
have claimed to be this Messiah. The most famous, of
course, was Jesus. His followers therefore gave him the title
Christ. *Mashiach*—the Hebrew word for Messiah—literally
means the "anointed." The Greek word for "anointed" is
Christos, and thus, Christ is really just another word for
Messiah.

Although Christians claim that Jesus was the Messiah
of the Jews, there are a number of important differences

26

between the way the Jew looks at the Messiah, and the way the Christian does. It is most important to know these differences.

THE JEWISH MESSIAH

The Jewish concept of the Messiah is that which is clearly developed by the prophets of the Bible. He is a leader of the Jews, strong in wisdom, power and spirit. It is he who will bring complete redemption to the Jewish people, both spiritually and physically. Along with this, he will bring eternal peace, love, prosperity, and moral perfection to the entire world.

The Jewish Messiah is truly human in origin. He is born of ordinary human parents, and is of flesh and blood like all mortals.

As described by the Prophet *(Isaiah 11:2)*, the Messiah is "full of wisdom and understanding, counsel and might, knowledge and the fear of G-d." He has a special feeling for justice, or, as the Talmud put it *(Sanhedrin 93b)*, he "smells and judges." He can virtually sense a man's innocence or guilt.

The Prophet *(Isaiah 11:4)* goes on to say that the Messiah will, "smite the tyrant with the rod of his mouth, and slay the wicked with the breath of his lips." Evil and tyranny will not be able to stand up before the Messiah.

Still, the Messiah is primarily a king of peace. Our Sages therefore teach us *(Derech Eretz Zuta:1):* "When the

Messiah is revealed to Israel, he will only open his mouth for peace. It is thus written *(Isaiah 52:7),* 'How beautiful upon the mountains are the feet of the messenger who announces peace.'"

The first task of the Messiah is to redeem Israel from exile and servitude. In doing so, he will also redeem the entire world from evil. Oppression, suffering, war and all forms of godlessness will be abolished. Mankind will thus be perfected, and man's sins against G-d, as well as his transgression against fellow man, will be eliminated. All forms of warfare and strife between nations will also vanish in the Messianic age.

Most important, the Jewish Messiah will bring all peoples to G-d. This is expressed most clearly in the *Alenu* prayer, which concludes all three daily services:

"May the world be perfected under the kingdom of the Almighty. Let all humans call upon Your Name and turn all the world's evildoers to You. Let everyone on earth know that every knee must bow to You . . . and let them all accept the yoke of Your kingdom."

We find a very similar thought in the High Holy Day *Amidah,* where we pray, "Let all creatures bow before You. May they form a single band to do Your will with a perfect heart."

The Jewish Messiah will thus have the task of perfecting the world. He will redeem man from servitude, oppression and his own evil. There will be great material prosperity in the world, and man will be restored to an Eden-like existence, where he can enjoy the fruits of the earth without toil.

In the Messianic age, the Jewish people will dwell freely in their land. There will be an "ingathering of the exiles," when all Jews return to Israel. This will eventually bring all nations to acknowledge the G-d of Israel and accept the truth of His teachings. The Messiah will thus not only be king over Israel, but, in a sense, ruler over all nations.

Ultimately, redemption comes from G-d alone, and the Messiah is only an instrument in His hands. He is a human being, consisting of flesh and blood like all mortals. He is, however, the finest of the human race, and as such, must be crowned with the highest virtues that mortal man can attain.

Although the Messiah may achieve the upper limit of human perfection, he is still human. The kingdom of the Jewish Messiah is definitely "of this world."

Judaism is a religion based on a people serving G-d. It is from the Jew that G-d's teachings emanate to all humanity. The redemption of Israel must therefore precede that of the rest of mankind. Before G-d redeems the world, He must redeem His oppressed, suffering, exiled and persecuted people, returning them to their own land and restoring their status.

The ultimate promise, however, is not limited to Israel alone. The redemption of the Jew is closely linked to the emancipation of all humanity as well as the destruction of evil and tyranny. It is the first step in man's return to G-d, where all mankind will be united into "a single band" to fulfill G-d's purpose. This is the "Kingdom of the Almighty" in the Messianic Age.

Although the Messiah may occupy a central place in this "Kingdom of Heaven," he is still not the primary figure. This position can only belong to G-d Himself.

This, in brief is the concept of the Jewish Messiah.

THE CHRISTIAN MESSIAH

The primary figure in Christianity is its Messiah. Its very name indicates that Christianity is completely based on the personality of the Messiah. As mentioned earlier, the name "Christ" comes from *Christos,* the Greek word for Messiah. The Christians are thus those who make the person of the Messiah central to their teachings.

The first major difference between the Jews and early Christians was that the Christians believed that the Messiah had already come, while the Jews believed that he was yet to come. At first, this was the main point of controversy.

The Jews had one major objection to the Christian Messiah, and that was the fact that he had been unsuccessful. Judaism had always taught that the Messiah would redeem Israel in a political sense, and Jesus had failed to accomplish this. Instead, he had been scourged and humiliated like a common rebel, and finally crucified along with two ordinary thieves.

How could the career of Jesus be reconciled with the glorious picture of the Messiah as taught by the Prophets of Israel? The early Christians faced this dilemma, and, in justifying Jesus as the Messiah, radically altered the entire concept. These new Messianic ideas were developed in the writing of John, and even more so in the Epistles of Paul.

If we look in these sources, we find a gradual transition. The Messiah of the Jew progressively becomes transformed into the Christ of the Christian. This can be traced in a series of logical steps.

1. Jesus was totally unsuccessful in redeeming the Jews politically, and therefore the early Christians could no longer look upon this as the task of the Messiah. His redemption had to be given a new meaning. They therefore taught that his mission was not to redeem man from political oppression, but only to redeem him from spiritual evil.

2. Once the Messiah's mission was redefined, it could also be expanded. Political oppression was a special problem of the Jews, but spiritual evil is worldwide. The early Christians therefore began to teach that Jesus had come to redeem the whole world. They rejected the view that he would come to redeem the Jewish people and their land first, and only then redeem the rest of the world. The Messiah's reign is therefore universal, but only spiritual. The kingdom of Jesus is thus "not of this world."

3. Jesus had been scourged and humiliated like a common rebel. His followers felt, however, that he had only preached repentence and good works, and therefore could

not be a common rebel. They were then faced with an important and difficult question. If Jesus was the true Messiah, then why did G-d allow him to undergo such frightful suffering? Why was he subjected to crucifixion, the most painful and shameful death of all? Why did G-d not save him from all this?

For his followers, there could only be one answer. The fact that Jesus was scourged, humiliated and crucified had to be the will of G-d. But still, another question remained. If Jesus did not sin, what purpose could there be in his suffering and death? For this, the early Christians found a most ingenious solution. The only answer could be that he suffered and died because of the sins of mankind.

But the question was still not completely answered. Had there not been suffering and death before this? Why did Christ himself have to suffer and die? What sin was so great that it required his sacrifice?

The early Christians answered that this was required to atone for the sin of Adam. All mankind is descended from Adam, and therefore, all inherit his sin. This "original sin" cannot be erased with good works, or even with ordinary human suffering. The only thing that could eliminate it was the death of Jesus.

The Messiah of the Christians therefore willingly went to a disgraceful and painful death in order that humanity might be redeemed from this "original sin." Mankind is therefore redeemed from evil, sin, suffering, death and the powers of Satan only by the blood of Christ.

Support for this belief was found in the 53rd chapter of
Isaiah, where the Prophet speaks of G-d's suffering servant,
who "bore the sin of many." Instead of interpreting it to
refer to the persecuted people, Israel, the early Christians
claimed that it referred to Jesus.

4. But still the question remained, how could the
career of the Redeemer end in such a shameful death? The
story had to be given a sequel. Such an epilogue was found
in another traditional Jewish belief, namely, that of the Res-
urrection of the Dead. The early Christians therefore taught
that Jesus had risen from the dead, and furthermore, that he
was the first one to do so. Therefore Jesus was not mortal
like other men.

5. Jesus' followers could not bring themselves to say
that G-d had forced this suffering and death upon His Messiah. Therefore, they had to say that the will of the Messiah
was exactly the same as the will of G-d, even when it came
to his crucifixion. But how could a mere mortal undertake
such suffering? The early Christians replied that Jesus was
not a mere mortal. Since his will was so uniquely related to
that of G-d, he had to be related to G-d in some special way.

6. During his lifetime, Jesus often spoke of G-d as "my
Father in Heaven." For the Jews, this was a common poetic
expression, and one that is still used in Jewish prayers. For
the pagan gentiles, however, it had a much more literal
connotation. The Greeks already had legends about men
who had been fathered by gods who had visited mortal
human women. Legends like these had even sprung up
about such eminent men as Plato, Pythagoras, and Alexan-

der the Great. Why should Jesus be any less? They therefore interpreted his poetic expression quite literally, to mean that he had an actual genetic relationship with G-d. Jesus therefore became the "son of G-d," conceived when the Holy Ghost visited Mary. As the "son of G-d," Jesus was not susceptible to sin or even death.

The death of Jesus was therefore only temporary. The only reason why it was needed at all was to atone for the sin of Adam. His followers taught that Jesus was resurrected for eternity and ascended to heaven. There he sits at the "right hand of G-d," even higher than the angels.

This was the first step toward the deification of Jesus, and it was not very difficult for the pagan world to take the second step. Jesus was credited with such statements as *(John 10:30)*, "I and the Father are one." He had also spoken of *(Matthew 28:19)*, "The Father, the Son, and the Holy Ghost." It was easy for the paganized Christians to look at the three as equal and identify Jesus with the "Son."

Jesus therefore became G-d-man—one person with two natures. He is G-d and man at the same time. Christians therefore soon found themselves speaking of Mary as the "mother of G-d."

7. Still, there were many Messianic prophecies that Jesus had failed to fulfill. The early Christians therefore taught that he would return to the world again in a "second coming." The Day of Judgement will then occur, and Jesus, having taken his seat at the "right hand of his Father," will judge every man who has ever lived. Those who believed in

him will be delivered, while those who did not will be eternally damned to hell.

It is only after this judgement that Satan will be conquered. Evil will then end, sin will vanish, and death will pass away. The powers of darkness will thus be eliminated, and the kingdom of heaven established.

8. In this world, meanwhile, all prayer must be addressed to Jesus. The Christian therefore concludes every prayer "in the name of Jesus Christ our Lord." In this sense, Jesus is the mediator between G-d and man.

*   *   *

This, in essence, is what the early Christians did to the Jewish concept of the Messiah. The Messiah ceased to be a mere man, and passed beyond the limits of mortality. They taught that man cannot redeem himself from sin, and therefore G-d, clothed in the form of the Messiah, had to freely shed his own blood to redeem mankind. Since Jesus did not fulfill the most important Messianic prophecies, they expected him to return to complete this task in a "second coming."

At first, Christians expected that this "second coming" would come very shortly, and prayed that they would see it in their lifetime. When their prayer was not answered, they began to hope that it would come a thousand years after Jesus' death. This was the millenium or "thousand year kingdom." Finally, after a thousand years passed and Jesus still had not returned, they postponed his "second coming" to an indefinite time.

We therefore see that the early Christians were forced to radically alter the Jewish concept of the Messiah in order to explain Jesus' failure. This, compounded with the pagan influence in the early church, gave birth to a Messianic concept totally alien to Judaism.

JEWISH REACTION

It is not very difficult to understand why the Jews totally rejected the contentions of Christianity.

First of all, the Jews had a tradition, well supported in the teachings of the Prophets, that the Messiah would bring about major changes in the world. The "spiritual kingdom" did not in any way fulfill these prophecies. The Jews were furthermore unconvinced by the answer of the "second coming," since it was not even hinted at in Biblical literature.

Thus, first of all, the Jew found absolutely no evidence to support Jesus' claim to having been the Messiah. On the other hand, Jesus' lack of success appeared to repudiate it.

Even more important, however, was the fact that the Christians had logically developed their belief in Jesus in such a manner that they radically altered many of the most basic Jewish beliefs. Even such a basic concept as G-d's unity was threatened by their teachings. Even if the evidence of Jesus' Messiahship were more concrete, its logical consequences would have to be rejected.

The early Christians tried to justify their contention by finding hints of it in the Jewish scriptures. They went over the entire Bible with a fine tooth comb, looking for any evidence however flimsy, to prove that Jesus was the Messiah, and that their entire logical structure was in accord with ancient Jewish teachings. In many cases, they were not above using verses out of context, changing texts, and even mistranslating them, in order to prove their point. One needs no further evidence than the fact that most modern Christian Bible scholars totally reject almost all the "proofs" of the early Christians. Indeed, some of the best refutations of these "proofs" may be found in contemporary Christian Bible commentaries.

Most important, Christianity tried to set itself up as the new "Israel," and looked upon the Jews as utterly rejected by G-d. It therefore taught that Judaism was a corrupt and dying religion, with little hope of growth or success.

The Jews, on the other hand, did much more than argue this point with words. They refuted it by embarking upon one of the most creative periods in their history. The entire scope of Talmudic literature was developed essentially during early post-Christian times.

Thus, to the Jew, the strongest refutation of Christianity was the fact that Judaism itself remained alive and vital. The Jew has found that he can both exist and flourish without accepting Christian beliefs. He believes that the Messiah is yet to come, and that at that time, the truth will become known and the Jew will be justified before all the world.

Although the Jews for Jesus movement is a relatively recent development in its present form, the groundwork for it was laid by the "ecumenical" movement. "Ecumenicism", however, does have ancient and, for the Jew, dangerous precedents.

ECUMENICISM AND DIALOGUE 1263 C.E.

——————— *by* ———————

BEREL WEIN

The winds of change that Vatican II unloosed into the Christian world are beginning to be felt. And even though the position of the Catholic Church vis-a-vis Jews and Judaism has yet to show any substantive, meaningful change, the new methodology of the Church regarding the treatment of the problem of the people of Israel has begun to emerge. The main bridge that the Church hopes to use in expanding a positive relationship with the Jewish people, particularly in the United States, is that of the open forum or dialogue. The Church is now much interested to foster open public discussion between Jews and Christians of the differences and similarities of the two major religions of Western man. In so doing, the Church has struck a responsive chord in certain Jewish circles, once again, particularly here in the United States. Unlike Orthodox Jewry, the agencies representing the Conservative, Reform and secular wings of Jewry have committed themselves to participation in this dialogue. (The exception of Orthodoxy is notable for two reasons. First, it is one of the few policy decisions that *all* of Orthodoxy is in accord with. Secondly, Orthodoxy's position is disturbing to both the Christian and non-orthodox Jewish participants; not to have the cooperation and blessing of the traditional Jew, whose participation, all feel, would give such an exchange real substance, lends a certain quality of hollowness to the dialogue.)

However, the idea of a "dialogue" between Jews and Christians is not a 20th Century thought but was already explored centuries ago, albeit in a different environment and under other circumstances.

The most famous example of an exchange of this order is the debate that took place in the city of Barcelona, Spain, in the year 1263. James I of Aragon sat on the throne of northern Spain, and the spirit of Christian dominance of the civilized world was wafted in the air. Seven hundred and four years have passed since then, but in the record of that dialogue written by Rabbi Mosheh ben Nachman (commonly called the Ramban, and, in the non-Jewish world, Nachmanides), and preserved by both Jewish and non-Jewish sources, one senses yet the grandeur and terror of that moment in Barcelona and a feeling of immediacy and relevancy overtakes the reader of that record. For here are our modern-day problems, differences, disputes, and bitterness poured out on an ancient canvas and curiously, the positions of the antagonists have changed very little in the seven centuries that have since swept by. It will be the attempt of this article to reflect some of the thoughts and words of this debate and thereby emphasize that the cascading dash to dialogue may perhaps be merely the foolish pursuit of an unattainable and ephemeral illusion.

THE HISTORICAL BACKGROUND

James I, who was destined to reign 63 years over the province of Aragon, was, as medieval monarchs went, a friend of the Jews. During the period of his reconquest of Catalonia and Aragon from the Moors, he consistently displayed a tolerance and sympathy towards the Jewish residents of those countries. He encouraged Jewish emigration to those lands, appointed Jews to vital governmental positions, and generally did nothing to interfere with the Jews' ability to practice and worship in the tradition of their fathers.[1]

However, then as now changes were being felt in the structure of the Roman Catholic Church, particularly in Spain. The reforms in the church initiated by Innocent III and continued by Gregory IX reached Spain and rested in the province of Aragon, where the "Holy Office" of the Inquisition was to reach dominance. The Dominican confessor to James I, Raymond de Penaforte, was noted for his zeal to punish, persecute, and/or convert the Jews in Aragon, and his influence over the king was notable.

From 1228 to 1250, a series of anti-Jewish economic edicts were issued by the king which helped foster a climate of anti-Jewish feeling in the land. In 1254, the famous trial of the Talmud in Paris occurred, and the Talmud was found guilty of stating calumnies against Christianity and cartloads of Talmudic manuscripts were burned by the order of

Louis IX of France. When this coercion had little or no effect on the Jews or on their reverence for the Talmud, the Dominican friars of Spain, benefitting by the lesson of their French colleagues, changed their strategy.

No longer was the Talmud criticized, it was rather extolled. The Midrosh now became an accepted source book of accurate portrayals, and Jewish scholarship was no longer publicly reviled. The reason for this was ingeniously simple—the truth of Christianity would now be proven, not from Christian or other non-Jewish sources, but rather from the Talmud and the Midrosh themselves! It was their obstructionism that prevented the Jews from seeing the light of Christianity emanating from their own holy books. This new approach was spearheaded by an apostate Jew who had become a leader in the Catholic church of Aragon, Pablo Christiani. Because of his zeal to convert his fellow Jews, he goaded Raymond, the king's confessor, to convince James to order a public debate regarding the proofs from the Talmud as to the veracity of Christianity. The burden of defending the Talmud and the Jews fell upon the venerable shoulders of one of the greatest of all Talmudists, Rabbi Mosheh ben Nachman. On the 20th of July in 1263, at the Court of James I of Aragon, this dialogue began. It was to last until the 31st of July, though actual debating sessions occupied only four days of this time. The shock of this debate was to leave scars on the memories of both protagonists which have lasted to this day.

THE DEBATE

The record of the debate that forms the basis for this article is one written by one of the protagonists himself—

the Ramban.[2] Written in a clear and lucid Hebrew style, it presents a picture of the debate and a record of the polemics as seen and heard by the Ramban.

At the outset, Mosheh ben Nachman insisted that he be granted the right of free speech throughout the debate. This right was guaranteed to him by the king, and because of this right, the Ramban at all times spoke boldly, incisively, and openly. It was the presence of this guarantee that made this medieval debate in reality a modern one wherein both sides speak their minds without intimidation. Such an open debate was a rarity in Christian Europe until our own times. Later events proved to the Ramban how costly the exercise of this freedom would prove to him personally. I would presume to state that this freedom of expression is what uniquely characterizes and ennobles this discussion and precludes any comparison with the earlier debate of Rabbi Yechiel of Paris[3] or the later encounter at Tortossa.[4] For here, perhaps for the only time in the annals of medieval Christian European history, Jew meets Gentile as equal, and for the majority of the debate is not the defendant or apologist but rather presses home his criticism and disbelief of Christian concepts and principles.

Rabbi Mosheh ben Nachman summarized one main historical argument against the acceptance of Christianity by the Jews of Aragon and, in so doing, he attempted to entirely avoid the necessity of debating Talmudic or Midrashic references to Jesus. "It has been proposed to me that the wise men of the Talmud themselves believed that Jesus was the Messiah, and that he was a man and a god, and not merely a mortal man alone. But is it not a well known fact that the incidents and events of Jesus occurred at the time of the Second Temple and that he was born and died before the destruction of that Temple? (70 C.E.) And the Rabbis of the Talmud, such as Rabbi Akiva and his colleagues, died after the destruction of the Temple . . . and the editor of the Talmud, Rav Ashi, lived almost 400 years after the Temple's destruction. If it would be true that the wise men of the Talmud believed in Jesus and in the truth of his religion, how then did they themselves remain faithful to the religion and practices of the Jews? For they lived and died as Jews, they and their children and their disciples unto this very day. And they are the ones who have taught us the faith of Judaism, for we are all Talmudic Jews . . . And if they believed in Jesus, as you are trying to impute from their words, why did they not behave as Friar Paul (Pablo Christiani), who evidently understands their words better than they (and themselves convert)?"

His argument resounds through the halls of time—the classic answer of Jewish tradition: "If our forefathers, who witnessed Jesus, saw his works, and knew him, did not hearken unto him, how should we accept the word of our king (James I), who himself has no first-hand knowledge of Jesus, and was not his countryman as were our forefathers?" Here the Ramban puts into awful clarity the basic point of contention between Jews and Christians. The stubbornness of the Jew stems not from his "perfidy" but rather from the fact that he is convinced of the truth of his own belief and not the slightest convinced of the truth of Christian belief. The current Vatican schema on the Jews remains unclear as to whether Christianity has yet come to grips with this fact. For it does not yet specify the cause of the Jew's affirmation of the one and denial of the other—it merely hopes through better social relations to soften, if not to reverse, that affirmation and denial.

The Dominicans were not deterred from their purpose by the Ramban's onslaught. They brought numerous passages from Talmudic and Midrashic literature to prove the truth of their faith. The Ramban stated that he did not consider himself bound by the "agadoth" of the Talmud,[5] and therefore no proofs could be deduced from them. However, he said that even if he granted their accuracy, they in no way agreed with Christian thought or belief. His strength in swimming in the sea of the Talmud easily refuted his antagonists who were not nearly as erudite in the subject matter as he. And he used every opportunity to return to the offensive against his opponents. "Does not the prophet say regarding the Messiah 'that he shall reign from sea to sea and from the river to the ends of the earth' (Psalms 72:8)—and has not your empire (the Roman empire), declined since it accepted Christianity? Do not your enemies, the Moslems, rule over a greater empire than yours? And does not the prophet also say that at the time of Messiah 'they shall not teach their friends war, etc'? (Jeremiah 31:33) and is it not written (Isaiah 11:9) that then 'the world shall be full of knowledge of the Lord as the waters cover the sea'. . .? And from the days of Jesus till now, the entire world is full of robbery and pillaging, and the Christians have spilled more blood than any of the other nations, and they are also sexually immoral. How hard it would be for you, my great King, and for your knights, to survive if there would be an end to warfare!"

This indictment of the status of the Christian, or, as we call it today, the Western world, is even sharper in our time when over fifty million people have been destroyed by war in the past century alone, and when all of the economies of the great powers of the world rest on a foundation of defense spending and war preparation.

The Ramban further stated that the basic dispute between Christianity and Judaism is not regarding the messianic mission of Jesus himself as much as it is regarding the entire Christian concept of Divinity and belief. "Listen to me, my master, my king," said the Ramban, "Our contention and judgment with you is not primarily concerning the Messiah,[6] for you are more valuable to me than the Messiah. You are a king and he is a king. You are a Gentile king and he is a king of Israel, for the Messiah will only be flesh and blood as you are. When I serve my Creator under your sovereign rule, in exile, poverty, oppression and humiliated by the nations that constantly insult us, my reward for this service is indeed great: For I bring forth a voluntary sacrifice to G-d of my own being, and through this shall I merit a greater portion of the world to come. However, when there will be a king of Israel, abiding by my Torah, who shall rule over all the nations, then I shall be involuntarily compelled to retain my faith in the Torah of the Jews, and therefore my reward shall not be as great (as it is now). However, the main dispute and disagreement between the Christians and the Jews is in that you have some very sorry beliefs regarding the essence of Divinity itself." Thus did the Ramban emphasize clearly that the fundamental differences between Judaism and Christianity are not those of detail and history but rather those of definition and understanding of the nature of Divinity and His relation to man.

The question of Original Sin was also touched upon in this debate. Both Pablo and King James asserted that all

men had been condemned to Hell because of the original
sin of Adam, but that the advent of belief in Jesus had
released man from this state of eternal damnation. To this
the Ramban retorted with bitter irony: "In our province we
have a saying—He who wishes to lie should be sure that the
witnesses to the transaction are far away. There are many
punishments mentioned in regard to Adam and Eve—the
earth was cursed, thorns and thistles shall grow therefrom,
man shall earn his bread by the sweat of his brow, that man
shall return to the dust, and that woman shall suffer the pain
and travail of childbirth. All of these conditions yet exist to
this day, and anything tangible that can be evidenced, as the
alleviation of any of these conditions, has yet to appear,
even since the advent of your messiah. But the curse of
damnation to Hell, which Scripture nowhere records, this is
the punishment which you say was relieved (by Jesus coming), for this is the one matter which no one can disprove.
Send from your midst someone, and let him return and
report to us! G-d forbid that the righteous should be punished in Hell for the sin of the first man, Adam. For my soul
is as equally related to the soul of the wicked Pharoah as to
the soul of my father, and I shall not be punished by the
damnation of my soul because of the sins of that Pharoah.
The punishments that accrue to mankind because of the sin
of Adam were physical, bodily punishments. My body is
given to me by my father and mother, and therefore if it was
ordered that they be mortal and die, so will their children
forever be mortal and die, for such is the law of nature."
But, he stated, the soul of man, which is given to him by the
Eternal Creator, is not damned because of the sins of others,
even of his ancestors themselves, unless he himself continues in their evil ways.

The Ramban thereupon entered into a theological disputation regarding the theories of the Virgin Birth and the Trinity. He proved them not to be Jewish in origin and that therefore "the mind of no Jew could understand or accept them." He stated that "your words (regarding the Talmud and the Messiah) are therefore for naught, because this is the kernel of our disagreement, but if you wish to discuss the concept of Messiah, I will bow to your wishes." He told the king that "you believe this bitter thing regarding divinity (the Virgin Birth and the concept of the trinity) because you are born a Christian, the son of Christian parents, and you have been indoctrinated your entire life by priests who have filled your mind and marrow with this belief, and you now accept its truth, by basis of habit alone." His criticism of these tenets of the Roman Catholic faith placed in sharp focus the reason for the Jew's refusal to accept Christianity from its very onset. Its notion of G-d was, and is, foreign to Jewish tradition and logic. Nothing has yet occurred to change this status either for the Jew or the Christian.

The Debate ended rather abruptly. It was never formally closed, but the king recessed it, apparently out of fear of rioting by fanatical mobs stirred up by emotional sermons of certain Dominican friars.[7] The king himself took an active part in the debate and one is struck by the fairness and tolerance of James I. It was only the deceitful friars who distorted the teachings of the Talmud. He is quoted by the Ramban as having told him that "I have yet to see such a man as you, who, though being wrong, has yet made an excellent presentation of his position."[8] The Ramban also notes that he received a gift of three hundred coins from James, evidently as reimbursement for his expenses. The

Ramban states that "I departed from [the king] with great affection." Mosheh ben Nachman remained in Barcelona for over a week, and was present for a sermon in the Synagogue on the following Sabbath delivered by a Dominican priest, in the presence of King James, calling on the assembled Jews to convert to Christianity.[9]

The Dominicans, angered by the Ramban's successful defense, turned their wrath against him personally. He was sentenced to temporary exile from Aragon and had to pay a fine for speaking blasphemy. In his old age, broken by the ordeal of his persecution and by a vision of the sorrows that would yet befall the Jews in Spain, Rabbi Mosheh ben Nachman emigrated to the Land of Israel in the year 1267 and on its holy soil he expired shortly thereafter.

CONCLUSION

The importance of this encounter between the Jews and the Christian world is not to be minimized. It would be many centuries before Jews dared to speak so openly to their Christian fellow countrymen about the fundamental differences that separate them. To our very day, no other Jewish religious leader of the caliber of the Ramban, responsible and responsive to his faith and tradition, has ever presented our case. Those who presume to speak for Judaism in today's dialogues would do well to read the record of this dialogue seven centuries ago. I do not believe that the case for Jews and Judaism can be better stated, with as much candor, compassion and truth, than the manner in which it is reflected in the words of Rabbi Mosheh ben Nachman. Both Jew and Christian would profit by a study of that record from Barcelona before plunging headlong into any new dialogue or ecumencial discussion. The issues and the world itself has changed little from the days of James I of Aragon. Neither has the people of Israel.

The mountain of His holiness, His Holy Temple
standing on the heights of eternal hills,
That is Sinai, the glory of G-d that dwelled
upon it, thrills,

Let the nations proclaim His majesty and awe,
The voice of the Red Sea, never ending,
where His flock saw,

All of His wonders, miracles, beauty,
Cleanse yourselves, O ye nations and states
Raise up your son, give glory and honor to the Lord![10]

NOTES

1. Yitzhak Baer, "A History of the Jews in Christian Spain," Volume I, pp. 138–147.
2. Vikuach Haramban—Found in *Otzar Havikuchim* by J. D. Eisenstein, Hebrew Publishing Society, 1915 and *Kithvey Haramban* by Rabbi Charles D. Chavel, Mosad Horav Kook, 1963.
3. Rabbi Yechiel of Paris, one of the leaders of the school of the Tosafists, defended the Talmud against the accusations of Nicholas Donin, a Jewish apostate, before Louis IX of Paris in 1254.
4. Tortossa was the locale of a series of debates carried on by many Jewish Rabbis, foremost among them being Rabbi Yoseph Albo, against Dominican Theologians and a Jewish apostate, Joshua Halorki, in the years 1413–1414, which ended in disaster for the Jewish cause.
5. The Agadoth—literally, Tales—are the parables and traditional legends of the Talmud—usually with a moral or ethical message woven into their fabric. The term "Agadah" is used in contradistinction to "Halochah" which is the law or legal system of Torah.
   Whether or not the Ramban's point in this connection was actually his belief, or was merely a tactic used for this discussion, has been a matter of conjecture among Jewish scholars for considerable time.

6. See Rabbi Chavel's note in his *Kithvey Ramban,* wherein he quotes the statement of the Ramban in the Sefer Hageulah, that "even if we admit to ourselves that our sins and those of our fathers are so enormous that all hope of comforting us be lost, and that our exile will last till eternity—all of this will still not damage our belief in the fundamental precepts (of our Torah), for the ultimate reward to which we look forward is only in the world to come—the pleasure of our soul in Paradise, and our salvation from Hell; yet we still believe in our redemption (the Messiah), because it is a wellknown truth among those of great stature in Torah and prophecy."

7. Baer, History of the Jews in Christian Spain, Vol. I, p. 153. Also see the *Vikuach Haramban* where the Ramban himself makes mention of the "preachers who stir up the mob and bring terror to the world, and of many great priests and knights of the king's court, who have advised me not to speak evil against their religion. Also the Jews of this sector reported that they were told to warn me not to continue to do so."

8. An alternative reading of this statement in the Hebrew original is: "I have yet to see such a man as you, who though not being a legal advocate, has yet made an excellent presentation of his position."

9. The Ramban himself delivered a sermon-lecture in rebuttal, entitled, "The Torah of G-d Is Perfect," a copy of which is printed in the *Kithvey Haramban* mentioned in note 2 above.

10. The last stanza of a poem "From Thy Hand, Lord, Give Forth Honor," written by the Ramban in honor of the Pesach festival.

The Missionaries claim that Jesus fulfilled all the prophecies pertaining to the Messiah. The truth, however, is that he did not fulfill even one of the important prophecies. All the things that he fulfilled were in reality quite trivial.

WAS JESUS THE MESSIAH? LET'S EXAMINE THE FACTS

by

PINCHAS STOLPER

If Christians merely believed that Jesus was *their* messiah, this belief would be of little concern to us as Jews. Their claim, however, is not that he is the Christian Messiah, but *our* Messiah, the Messiah of the Jews, the Messiah foretold by the Jewish Prophets. Christians then attempt to prove this belief by quoting *our* Bible.

Certain Christian missionary groups have now set up a front organization called "Jews for Jesus," through which they entice naive Jews to Christianity with an old and discredited argument. "Don't become a Christian," they will argue, "remain a Jew,—however, while you remain a loyal Jew, accept Jesus as your "Messiah."

In view of the confusion created by the many false claims of missionary groups, Jews must be armed with the facts to substantiate our conviction that everything Christians claim for Jesus as the *Jewish* Messiah is false.

The following few "items" will point out some of the glaring discrepancies and inconsistancies in the missionaries' arguments:—

Item: The Jewish Messiah is to be a human being born naturally to husband and wife. He is not to be a god, nor a man born of supernatural or virgin birth, as the Christians claim.

Nowhere does our Bible say that the Messiah would be a god or G-d-like. The very idea that G-d would take on human form is repulsive to Jews because it contradicts our concept of G-d as being above and beyond the limitations of the human body and situation. Jews believe that G-d *alone* is to be worshipped, not a being who is His creation, be he angel, saint, or even the Messiah himself.

Nowhere does the Bible predict that the Messiah will be born to a virgin. In fact, virgins never give birth anywhere in the Bible. This idea is to be found only in pagan mythology. To the Jewish mind, the very idea that G-d would plant a seed in a woman is unnecessary and unnatural. After all,—what is accomplished by this claim? What positive purpose does it serve? The claim that Mary did not have natural relations with her husband must have made the Jews of that time suspect her of wrong-doing. The New Testament (the Christian Bible) admits as much when it says (Matthew 1,19), "Then Joseph her (Mary's) husband, being a just man, and not willing to shame her in public, decided to divorce her quietly." The whole idea of virgin birth serves no purpose, except to attract pagans to Christianity.

Item: The Jewish Messiah is expected to return the Jews to their land. Jesus was born while the Jews still lived in their land, before they had gone into exile. He could not restore them to their land because they were still living in it!

Item: The true Messiah is to rebuild the Temple in Jerusalem—but Jesus lived while the Temple was still standing.

Item: The Jewish Bible says that the Messiah will redeem Israel. In the case of Jesus, the very opposite took place. Not long after his death, the Holy Temple in Jerusalem was destroyed, Jerusalem was laid to waste, and the Jews went into exile to begin a 1900 year long night of persecution,—largely at the hands of the followers of this self-styled "Messiah"!

Item: The Prophets in the Bible foretold (Isaiah 45 and Zafania 3) that when the Messiah comes, all the nations of the world will unite to acknowledge and worship the one true G-d. "The knowledge of G-d will fill the earth. The world will be filled with the knowledge of G-d as the waters cover the seas" (Isaiah 11,9). Nothing of this nature took place following the death of Jesus. On the contrary, Islam developed and became the religion of the Arabs and many other nations, Christianity broke up into many conflicting sects which were constantly at war with each other, and a large part of the world continued to worship idols. Even today the world is far from the worship of one G-d.

Item: When the true Messiah comes, his influence will extend over all peoples who will worship G-d at the Temple

in Jerusalem. The Prophet says, "For My House will become the House of Prayer for all the Nations." This has
obviously not yet taken place, and, therefore, the Messiah
has not yet come.

Item: During the time of the Messiah a new spirit will
rule the world, and man will cease committing sins and
crimes; this will especially apply to the Jews. The Torah (in
Deuteronomy 30,6) says that "G-d will circumcise your
heart and the heart of your children to love G-d." The
Prophets taught: "And your people are all righteous, they
will inherit the earth forever." (Isaiah 60, 21); "In that day I
will seek the sins of Israel and there will be none." (Jeremiah
50,20); "I will give you a new heart and a new spirit—and
you will obey my laws and commandments and do them."
(Ezekiel 36,21). Soon after the time of Jesus, ignorance of
G-d and even ignorance of science and philosophy filled the
earth, as the "Dark Ages" overtook the world.

Item: The true Messiah is to reign as King of the
Jews. Jesus' career as described in the New Testament lasted
all of three years, at the end of which he was crucified by the
Romans as a common criminal. He never functioned as
anything but a wandering preacher and "faith healer;" certainly, he held no official position or exercised any rule of
any kind.

Item: During the time of the Messiah, prophecy will
return to the Jewish people and the presence of G-d will
dwell amongst us. (Ezekiel 37,27); "And after that I will
pour my spirit on all of mankind and your sons and daughters will prophesy." These predictions, too, are yet to be
fulfilled.

Item: One of the Messiah's major tasks is to bring peace to the entire world. In the time of the Messiah, there are to be no more wars, and the manufacture of arms will cease. The Prophet Isaiah (2,4) says, "And they shall beat their swords into plow shares and their spears into pruning hooks. Nation shall not lift up sword against nation, neither shall they learn war any more." Yet, Christian nations are very war-like, and wars have been going on almost non-stop since the time of Jesus up to and including today.

Item: The New Testament itself claims that the prophecies concerning the Messiah were to be realized in Jesus' own generation. Mark (13,30) clearly says, "Truthfully I say unto you that this generation shall not pass till all these things be done." In Matthew 4, Jesus is quoted as saying that "The Kingdom of Heaven is at hand." 2,000 years have passed and still nothing has been accomplished.

Item: Nowhere does the Jewish Bible say that the Messiah would come once, be killed, and return again in a "second coming." The idea of a second coming is a pure rationalization of Jesus' failure to function in any way as a messiah, or to fulfill any of the prophecies of the Torah or the Prophets. The idea is purely a Christian invention, with no foundation in the Bible.

Item: The Bible says that the Messiah would be descended in a direct line from King David. However, if G-d was Jesus' "father," is it not somewhat ridiculous to claim that he is descended from King David on his father's side?

Item: Why do some Missionaries insist on distorting the meaning of the words of the prophets in order to substantiate their claims? (An example: the Hebrew term in Isaiah "almah" which means a "young woman" is mistranslated as "virgin.") Honest Christian scholars now acknowledge that this is "a pious fraud" and now (see the new Protestant "Revised Standard Version" of the Bible) translate the word correctly. This is but one of many mistranslations or forced translations.

Item: While on the cross Jesus is quoted as saying, "Forgive them Father, for they (the Jews) know not what they do." Why do some Christians insist on persecuting the Jews if Jesus *himself* gave instructions to forgive them?

But further—if his rising from the dead was so crucial to demonstrate who he was, why did this take place in secret and not in the presence of his "thousands" of devotees?

Item: Jesus claimed that he did not intend to change the Laws of Moses,—"Think not that I have come to abolish the Law (Torah) and the Prophets, I have come not to abolish them but to fulfill them. For truly, I say to you, till heaven and earth pass away, not an iota, not a dot, will pass from the Law until all is accomplished. Whoever then breaks one of the least of these commandments and teaches men so, shall be called least in the Kingdom of Heaven." (Matthew 5). Later on, he himself abrogated some of the laws, while his followers eventually abolished or changed nearly all of them.

However, the Torah itself clearly states in many places that its laws are eternal, never to be abolished. And even the Christians acknowledge that the Jewish Bible is the word of G-d. If the Torah is eternal and Jesus himself claims to have no intention of abolishing or changing it, why do the Christians celebrate the Sabbath on Sunday when G-d clearly calls the Saturday-Sabbath an Eternal Covenant? Why do Christians eat pig when the Torah forbids it? What reason can Christians give for not celebrating Rosh Hashana and Yom Kippur which are clearly spelled out in the Torah? This same argument applies to hundreds of other Torah laws that are ignored by Christians.

On the other hand, Christmas and Easter are not mentioned in either the Jewish Bible or the Christian "New Testament,"—these festivals are pagan in origin, adapted for Christian use. But Pesach, Sukkos and Shavuos are clearly spoken of in the Bible. On top of which, Jesus nowhere requests that the Biblical festivals no longer be observed.

Item: Christians teach the philosophy of "turning the other cheek" and "loving your enemy." Do you know of any Christian nations that live by this impractical ethic, or even take it seriously?

Item: The many Christian statements about G-d being "Love" have been borrowed from the Jewish Bible and the Jewish religion. Among many such quotations from our Torah are: "Love thy neighbor as thyself"; "Love the stranger, for you were strangers in the land of Egypt"; "And you shall love the L-rd thy G-d with all your heart and with all your soul and with all your might."

If G-d is "Love," how can Christians explain the silence and indifference of the Church and most Christian nations while six million Jews were being gassed and burned by the

Germans? Why the stone-like silence during the Six Day War? Where was Christian love during the Spanish Inquisition and the hundreds of pogroms inspired by priests and monks?

Item: Judaism believes that G-d is eternal, above and beyond time. G-d cannot be born, He cannot die, He cannot suffer, He can not "become flesh", nor can He be divided into sections. ("Father, Son, and Holy Ghost") These are pagan notions. Certainly no "G-d" or "Son of G-d" could have called out on the cross, as Jesus is supposed to have said, "My G-d, my G-d, why have you abandoned me?" If he was G-d's son, he would at least have said, "My father . . ."

Item: If Jesus was really the Messiah, why does the New Testament admit that all the rabbis of the time, without one exception, rejected his claim? Why was there not one man of learning, nor one prominent leader who accepted him?

Item: If Jesus was the Messiah, why did the overwhelming majority of his own people, the Jews living at that time, reject him? Why did his followers consist of a handful of people, almost all of whom were poorly educated? Why did his own family turn against him?

Who was in a position to judge if he was or was not the Messiah—his own people, who anxiously awaited the arrival of the Messiah, or pagan peoples who had no understanding of what the concept really meant?

Item: Jesus commanded his disciples to preach to the Jews only and not to the Gentiles (Matthew 10), yet his disciples disobeyed him and did just the opposite. He clearly thought of himself as the Messiah of the Jews and of no one else. Yet, he was accepted by foreign nations and not by the Jews.

Item: If God has "rejected" the Jews for not "accepting Jesus" as Christians claim, why have we managed to survive 2,000 years of Christian persecution? How do Christians explain the miracle of Jewish survival? Why has G-d restored the city of Jerusalem and the Land of Israel to His "rejected" people?

How do they explain the fact that the Jewish people has re-established its national life in its ancient homeland, and is in possession of the City of Jerusalem? These are living historic facts without parallel. Must not the Christians now acknowledge that the re-emergence of a Jewish State is indeed an unfolding and realization of Bible prophesy in our day? Does this not demonstrate that the many Biblical prophecies that speak of the return of the Jew to his land refers to the Jews and not to anyone else? (The Christians often refer to themselves as the "real Jews"—the "New Israel," i.e. G-d chose them because the Jews rejected Jesus.)

Isn't this theological "slap in the face" the reason for the Pope's refusal to recognize Israel, and for Christian silence during the Six Day War?

Item: The Prophets contain many prophecies concerning the end of days and the time of the Messiah that have not yet taken place. These *will* all take place when the Messiah comes.

Why do we need a Messiah in the first place? In order to teach the Torah to the world and to establish "The Kingdom of G-d on Earth." If the Christians have done away with the laws of the Torah, if they no longer regard the Torah as valid, what is left to teach mankind? Nowhere does the Torah suggest that it is to be abolished by the Messiah. On the contrary, the Torah is eternal, and the purpose of the Messiah is to bring us to the day when all of the Jewish people will observe the Torah and all of mankind will acknowledge its truths.

Item: Nowhere does the Torah state that someone else's death can bring forgiveness to a person's sins. On the contrary, each man will be punished for his sins, and each man must repent for his sins alone. "The soul that sinneth it shall die"; "Sons will not be punished for the sins of their fathers." The idea that someone else's death 1,900 years ago can somehow bring forgiveness from G-d for my sins is absurd and unfounded. Each person must return to G-d, each sinner must change his own ways and seek G-d's forgiveness.

*   *   *

Jews firmly believe that the Messiah will come. We believe that man will not self-destruct, that we will not disappear in a gigantic atomic blast. Man is basically good, and G-d's Kingdom will be established. However, it is not enough to believe in G-d. Faith alone is not adequate,—G-d demands deeds and action. G-d's revelation on Mount Sinai demands obedience to the 613 commandments spelled out in the written and unwritten Torah. G-d wants discipline, loyalty, and practice; not pious statements and magical formulas. Jews wait for the day when "G-d will be King over all the earth and on that day He will be One and His name One." (Zacharia 14,9).

Maimonides put our belief into words—and we firmly stand by these words, "I firmly believe, in complete faith, in the coming of the Messiah, and although he may tarry, I daily wait for his coming." Indeed, the Messiah is coming. . . . we can almost hear his footsteps.

In the First Corinthians (9:20), the apostle Paul says, "Unto the Jews, I come as a Jew, that I might convert the Jews. To those who believe in the Law, I come like one who follows the Law, that I might convert those who follow the Law." When the Missionaries approach us, they come as Jews, quoting from our Bible. It is both interesting and instructive to carefully examine a few of their "proofs".

JESUS AND THE BIBLE
by
ARYEH KAPLAN

For almost two thousand years, Christians have been trying to convince the Jews that they are right.

After all, Jesus was a Jew, and it seems strange that his own people refused to accept him.

One of the favorite ploys of the missionaries is to attempt to use the Jewish Bible to prove that Jesus was the Messiah of the Jews.

It takes a lot of nerve for outsiders to tell us how to interpret *our* Bible, written in *our* language.

Jews also know how to read the Bible. It was originally given in Hebrew, which is our language. When the Christians translated the Bible, they often slanted their translations to suit their own purposes. A close look at the original

62

Hebrew is enough to destroy a good portion of their "proofs."

In many cases we do not even have to go to the original Hebrew. Merely taking the passages in context does away with all their "proof."

Let us take a few examples:

*   *   *

Missionaries claim that Jesus fulfilled the prophecy of the Messiah being born in Bethlehem.

They base this on the verse (Michah 5:1), "But you, Bethlehem Ephratah, which are little among the thousands of Judah. Out of you shall one come forth unto Me, to be a ruler in Israel."

Both Matthew (2:6) and John (7:43) attempt to use this as proof that Jesus was the Messiah.

Of course, this does not prove anything, since thousands of children were born in Bethlehem.

Furthermore, if this is really speaking of Jesus, why was he never accepted as a "ruler in Israel."

The verse continues to say (Michah 5:4), "And there shall be peace."

This means to say that the Messiah will bring peace to the world, as we find elsewhere in the Bible (Isaiah 2:4).

If this is speaking of Jesus, why did he not succeed in bringing peace to the world?

He himself said that he is not coming to bring peace but the sword (Matthew 10:34).

But if this verse (Micah 5:1) is actually speaking of the true Messiah, then it is really referring to a descendant of King David. Since David came from Bethlehem (1 Samuel 17:12), the Bible speaks of Bethlehem as the Messiah's place of origin.

The true Messiah, who Jews are still waiting for, will be a ruler and will bring lasting peace to the world.

*   *   *

Missionaries claim that Jesus fulfilled a prophecy that the Messiah would be born of a virgin.

They attempt to prove this from a verse, which even many contemporary Christian editions of the Bible translate to read (Isaiah 7:14), "Therefore, the L-rd Himself shall give you a sign: Behold a young woman shall conceive and bear a son, and shall call his name Immanuel."

The idea of gods and demigods being born of virgins occurs in many places in pagan mythology.

When Matthew (1:23) quoted this passage and translated it into the Greek of the New Testament, his anxiety to prove a point led him to actually mistranslate this passage.

He translates the Hebrew word *Alma,* which actually means "young woman" as "virgin." Thus, we suddenly have an instant prediction of the virgin birth of the Messiah.

But the proper Hebrew word for virgin is *Besulah,* and *Alma* is never translated as "virgin."

More honest recent Christian Bible translations, such as the Revised Standard Version, the Jerusalem Bible, and the New English Bible, have corrected this original error.

Furthermore, there is absolutely no evidence that this prophecy speaks of the Messiah at all. It was directed at King Ahaz, and, according to most Biblical commentators, speaks of the birth of King Hezekiah rather than of the Messiah.

* * *

Missionaries claim that Jesus fulfilled the prophecy of being a prophet like Moses.

G-d says in the Bible (Deuteronomy 18:18), "I will raise them up a prophet among their brethren, like unto you (Moses)." What this verse means in context is that any prophet must be similar in qualifications to Moses, i.e. Jewish, a scholar, righteous, and of the highest personal character.

But John (1:45) and the book of Acts (3:22, 7:37) take this quote out of context, claiming that this verse refers to Jesus, and gives him the right to contradict the Torah of Moses.

However, this is an obvious distortion, since the Bible openly states that there would never be another prophet like Moses (Deuteronomy 34:10), "And there shall not arise a prophet in Israel like unto Moses."

G-d Himself attested to Moses, as we find (Exodus 19:9), "And G-d said to Moses: Behold, I come to you in a thick cloud, that the people may hear when I speak with you, and may believe in you forever."

At Mount Sinai, G-d attested to the prophecy of Moses by publicly speaking to him in the presence of millions of people. He never did the same for Jesus.

Indeed, there is no evidence that Jesus was a prophet at all, in Jewish terms.

The Bible (Deuteronomy 18:22) says that one of the signs of a true prophet is when his prophecy comes true exactly. There is no evidence that Jesus fulfilled this condition (See John 9:29).

Furthermore there is no evidence that the original passage (Deuteronomy 18:18) speaks of the Messiah at all. The verse merely states that the future prophets of Israel in general would share Moses' saintly qualities.

* * *

Missionaries claim that Jesus fulfilled the prophecy of living a sinless life.

They base this on the verse (Isaiah 53:9), "And they

made his grave with the wicked, and with the rich his tomb, although he had done no violence, neither was any deceit in his mouth."

This is the famous "Suffering Servant" passage in Isaiah.

Some commentators indeed state that this passage is speaking of the Messiah. Others, however, say that it is speaking of the entire Jewish people. A careful reading of the entire passage may well convince you that it is speaking of the Six Million Jews killed by Hitler. Other commentators say that it is speaking of the Prophet Isaiah himself.

In any case it cannot be proven that this passage is speaking of the Messiah at all.

Furthermore, Jesus himself was far from being sinless as the Gospel claims.

Speaking to the entire Jewish people, G-d commanded us to keep the Sabbath in the Ten Commandments. Since G-d himself gave this commandment, no one can abrogate it.

Yet, the Gospel records that Jesus violated the Sabbath.

As expected, the people's reaction was one of outrage. The Gospel records that the people said (John 9:16). "This fellow is no man of G-d, he does not keep the Sabbath." They realized that "miracles" alone do not give anyone the right to go against G-d, as G-d Himself warned in the Bible

(Deuteronomy 13:2). Only the gullible and superstitious are taken in by "miracles" and magic alone.

Beyond this, the Gospel records many instances where Jesus claimed to be G-d (John 10:30, 14:9, 16:15). If so, from the Jewish point of view, he was guilty of idolatry, one of the worst possible sins.

*   *   *

Missionaries claim that Jesus fulfilled the prophecy that the Messiah would be killed by crucifixion.

They quote a Biblical verse, which, correctly translated, reads (Psalm 22:17), "For dogs have encompassed me, a company of evil-doers have enclosed me, *like a lion,* they are at my hands and feet."

"Like a lion" in Hebrew is *KeAri.* The fundamentalist Christian interpreters actually changed the spelling of the word from *KeAri* to *Kari.* If one then totally ignores Hebrew grammar, one can twist this to mean "He gouged me." Then, as in the King James' Version, they make this verse read "they pierced my hands and feet."

However, this bears no relation to the original meaning of the verse. Even with the change in spelling, it is a forced translation.

This is but one more example of the lengths missionaries go to prove that they are right.

Furthermore there is absolutely no evidence that this

Psalm is speaking of the Messiah. From the opening verse, it would seem that King David, the author of this Psalm, was actually speaking of himself.

* * *

Missionaries claim that Jesus fulfilled the prophecy of dying for our sins.

The Bible says (Isaiah 53:11), "He shall see the travail of his soul . . . who by his knowledge did justify the Righteous One to the many, and their iniquity he did bear."

We are again in the famous "Suffering Servant" passage.

Missionaries claim that it teaches that our sins can only be forgiven through Jesus. This is a basic Christian doctrine.

However, the Bible clearly states (Deuteronomy 24:16), "The fathers shall not die for the children, neither shall the children die for the fathers; every man shall die for his own sin."

Every man is responsible for his own actions, and he himself must make them good. This is a most basic theme repeated over and over in the Bible.

According to the commentaries who say that the "Suffering Servant" is the Messiah (or the prophet Isaiah), a more precise translation would indicate that he did not suffer *to atone* for our sins, but suffered *because of* our sins.

The Messiah's mission is to perfect mankind. The more we sin, the more difficult we make his task. Thus, our sins will cause the Messiah great anguish.

According to the commentators who contend that the "Suffering Servant" is the entire Jewish people it is not very far fetched to say that the prophet is speaking of the Six Million who died for the sins of mankind.

Missionaries lay great stress on the fact that the Bible prescribes blood as atonement (Leviticus 17:11). They therefore claim that without the blood of Jesus, there can be no remission of sin (Hebrews 9:22).

However, there is no place where the Bible says that blood is the *only* means of atonement. Furthermore a close reading of the chapters on sacrifices shows that the sacrificial blood was only prescribed for a small category of transgressions.

There is one way of atonement, however, repeated again and again in the Bible. This is repentance. (See Ezekiel 33:11, 33:19, Jeremiah 36:3, etc.) The prophet said (Hosea 14:3), "Take with you words, and return to G-d." The main way back to G-d is through words of prayer. The sacrificial blood might have helped in some cases, but the most important part of atonement was always repentence and prayer.

It is not overly difficult to approach G-d. But it does involve effort on the part of the individual.

* * *

There are many other "proofs" offered by the missionaries. Every one is as twisted as those presented above, but to refute each one would require an entire book.

The main thing is that a clear reading of the Jewish Bible offers absolutely no support to the "proofs" of Christianity. In most cases, all you need is a good translation (or better still, the Hebrew original), and all those "proofs" fall away. Many contemporary Christian scholars admit as much.

However, the missionaries never mention the most important prophecies concerning the Messiah that Jesus *did not* fulfill.

The main task of the Messiah was to bring the world back to G-d, and to abolish all war, suffering and injustice from the world. Clearly, Jesus did not accomplish this.

In order to get around this failure on the part of Jesus, Christians invented the doctrine of the "Second Coming" (Hebrews 9:29, Peter 3). All the prophecies that Jesus did not fulfill the first time are supposed to be taken care of the second time around. However, the Jewish Bible offers absolutely no evidence to support the Christian doctrine of a "Second Coming."

Anything that they can twist to prove that Jesus was the Messiah is exploited to the fullest. All the embarrassing prophecies that he did not fulfill are swept under the rug of a "Second Coming."

The prophecies that Jesus is said to have fulfilled are, for the most part, trivial. It really does not make much difference in G-d's plan if the Messiah is born in Bethlehem or conceived by a virgin. His really important mission is to perfect the world. This, Jesus failed to do.

Jesus, therefore, was not the Messiah of the Jewish tradition.

We still await the true Messiah who will accomplish all this in his first attempt.

But, many argue, even if Jesus was not the Messiah, he was still a perfect human being, and one that we may take as an example. A closer look at his career, however, raises many questions about his "perfection".

BEHOLD THE MAN:
THE REAL JESUS
by
ARYEH KAPLAN

Many people are fascinated by the person of Jesus. Even when they find it impossible to accept Christian theology, they still feel that they can identify with Jesus the person. They see him as someone who preached love and peace, and whose life embodied the greatest ideals.

When we look at Jesus in such idealized terms, many of the things done in his name seem very strange. How could the Crusaders have pillaged and destroyed entire communities in his name? How could the Inquisition have tortured people to death in the name of a man who taught that the foremost commandment was "love your neighbor as yourself"? How are such contradictions possible?

It is much less surprising that his followers did not live by Jesus' teachings when we realize that even Jesus himself did not abide by them. Christians like to present us with an idealized picture of Jesus the man, but a careful reading of the Gospels dispells this picture very quickly.

Let us look at a few examples.

One of the best known teachings of Jesus is *(Luke 6:29)*, "If someone smites you on one cheek, turn the other cheek." This might have been a beautiful ideal, but Jesus himself did not live up to it. When one of the High Priest's officers struck him, Jesus did not turn the other cheek at all. Instead, the Gospel tells us that his response was *(John 13:23)*, "if I spoke amiss, state it in evidence at my trial. If I spoke well, then why did you smite me?" He did not meekly and quietly submit, as he himself is alleged to have preached.

Throughout history, it seems that the only one who ever "turned the other cheek" was the Jew.

In the Sermon on the Mount, Jesus instructed his followers *(Matthew 5:43)* "Love your enemies, bless those who curse you, and do good to those who hate you." This might have been a fine lesson if Jesus himself lived up to it. But when it came to his own enemies, Jesus declared *(Luke 19:27)*, "Take my enemies, who would not have me rule over them, bring them here, and kill them before me."

Jesus might have preached against vindictiveness, but he did not practice as he preached, when he said *(John 11:39)*, "I come to the world for judgement. I may give sight to the sightless, but I will blind those who see."

Some of us may have a picture of Jesus preaching love and peace, as when he said *(Matthew 5:22)*, "Anyone who nurses anger against his brother must be brought to judgement . . . If he even sneers at him, he will have to answer for it in the fires of hell." The picture, however, changes very rapidly when Jesus himself is put to the test. We then find him declaring *(Matthew 10:34)*, "Think not that I have come to send peace to the world. I come not to send peace, but the sword."

Jesus subjected anyone who dared oppose him to the most awful abuse, curses and threats of dire punishment. When the Jews tried to defend their ancient faith, Jesus answered them by saying, *(Matthew 23:33)*, "You snakes, you generation of vipers, how can you escape the damnation of hell?"

Jesus did not limit himself to his immediate opponents, such as the Rabbis and teachers. He spoke against all those who dared not believe in him, branding them as outcasts subject to divine punishment. We thus hear his pronouncement *(John 3:36)*, "He who believes in the Son has everlasting life. But he who does not believe in the Son shall not see life, but shall suffer the everlasting wrath of G-d." He may have preached love, but it was a very restricted love. He thus said *(John 3:5)*, "I surely say to you: Unless a man is born of water and the Spirit, he cannot enter the Kingdom of G-d."

In contrast to this, the Rabbis, whom Jesus hated so much, did not place any such limitations on G-d's love. It was the Rabbis of the Talmud who made the statement *(Tosefta, Sanhedrin 13)*, "The righteous of all nations have a share in the World to Come." They saw G-d's love as available to all people, and not only to Jews.

An even stronger statement can be found in our Midrashic literature, where a rabbi declares *(Tana DeBei Eliahu Rabbah 9),* "I call heaven and earth as witnesses: Any individual, whether gentile or Jew, man or woman, servant or maid, can bring the Divine Presence upon himself in accordance with his deeds."

The Jewish attitude toward non-Jews is most clearly expressed in King Solomon's prayer, where he says *(I Kings 8:41–43),* "When a stranger, who is not of Your people Israel, but comes from a distant land . . . turns in prayer toward this Temple, then listen to his prayers."

Jesus, however, was not so broad minded. When he sent out his twelve disciples, he charged them *(Matthew 10:5, 6),* "Do not take the road to gentile lands, and do not enter any Samaritan city. Go only to the lost sheep of Israel."

The Rabbis who lived in Jesus' time taught *(Avos 4:3),* "Do not despise any man." They likewise declared *(Baba Kama 38a),* "Even a gentile who studies Torah is equal to a High Priest." These Rabbis saw G-d's salvation freely available to all men. Contrast this with the terrible sentence proclaimed by Jesus *(John 15:6),* "He who does not abide in me is thrown away like a withered branch. Such withered branches are gathered together, cast into the fire and burned." This terrible statement was later used by the Catholic Church to justify their practice of burning nonbelievers at the stake.

In the Sermon on the Mount, Jesus preached *(Matthew 5:43:44)*, "You have been previously taught to love your neighbor and hate your enemy. But I say to you: Love your enemies and bless those who curse you." Jesus may have said this, but the Gospels are aflame with his own words of hatred toward those who did not accept him. Time after time, he displays the same appetite for revenge as any other mortal.

One of the basic teachings of Judaism is *(Leviticus 18:19)*, "You shall love your neighbor as yourself." This commandment is so important that Rabbi Akiva declared that it was the fundamental principle of the Torah. Even though this is openly stated in the Torah, written over a thousand years before Jesus' birth, many people still think of it as one of Jesus' teachings.

But even in explaining this commandment of love, Jesus was not above displaying his vindictiveness. The Gospel *(Luke 19:29)*, records that he was asked, "But who is my neighbor?" Jesus replied with one of the best known parables in the Gospels:

A man traveling from Jerusalem to Jericho is attacked by robbers. They plunder and beat him, leaving him half dead by the roadside. A priest comes along and sees the injured man, but he promptly crosses the road to avoid him. A Levite then happens to pass by, and he also crosses the road to avoid him. Finally a Samaritan comes by and is touched by pity. He binds the stranger's wounds, carries him to a secure spot, and tenderly cares for him. Thus, the Samaritan becomes the perfect example of the good neighbor.

At first glance, this looks like a most beautiful story. But when we look beneath the surface, we see Jesus' vindictiveness only too clearly.

Let us carefully note the three persons who saw the unfortunate victim. They are a priest *(Cohen)*, a Levite and a Samaritan. Anyone familiar with the three classes of Jews called to the Torah, knows that they are Cohen (priest), Levite and Israelite. We would therefore expect that after the Cohen and Levite passed up the victim, the story would tell us that the third person was an Israelite, an ordinary Jew.

Instead, however, Jesus substitutes a Samaritan, a member of a tribe who had been enemies with the Jews for almost five hundred years. This Samaritan then becomes the example of moral love. The Priests and Levites, who were the religious leaders of the Jews, were thus downgraded, while the hated Samaritan was praised. What Jesus is implying is that every Jew, even a religious leader, is incapable of even a simple act of mercy.

Even in his parable about love, Jesus was not above demonstrating his spite toward the Jewish leaders who rejected him. "Good Samaritan" is a byword among Christians to this very day. Many churches even bear the name, "Church of the Good Samaritan." But Jesus' vindictiveness assured that there would never be a church with the name, "Church of the Good Israelite."

Jesus was even able to be vindictive against a tree. When he found himself hungry, he was not able to restrain his too human emotions. The Gospel thus records (Matthew 21:18, 19), "In the morning, on his way to the city, Jesus felt hungry. Seeing a fig tree near the road, he went up to it, but found nothing on it but leaves. He said to the tree, 'may you never bear fruit anymore.' The tree then withered and died." The Gospel of Mark *(11:13)* makes it plain that it was not even the season for figs.

Did this innocent tree deserve such cruel punishment? It was not even the season for figs, and the tree was merely fulfilling its nature. If Jesus merely wanted to show his miraculous powers, as the gospel seems to indicate, why did he not command the tree to bring forth fruit?

Indeed, the Talmud *(Taanis 24a)* brings a very similar incident, but with a very different ending. Rabbi Yosi's son once wanted to provide his father's field hands with food. All he could find was a fig tree, but it was not the season, and the tree was bare. He cried out, "Fig tree, fig tree, send forth your fruit so that my father's workers may eat." The Talmud tells us that the tree produced fruit before its time and the men were able to fill themselves.

If Jesus were truly capable of miracles, he could have done the same. Instead, he chose to display his vindictiveness.

A primary teaching of Judaism is expressed by the Psalmist many generations before Jesus. He declared *(Psalm 145:9),* "G-d is good to all, and his love extends over all His works." No distinction is made between Jew and gentile.

Contrast this with the following event in Jesus' career *(Mark 2:25-27):* "A woman whose daughter was possessed by an unclean spirit heard of Jesus, and came in, falling at his feet. She was a Gentile, a Phoenician from Syria. She begged Jesus to drive out the spirit from her daughter. Jesus replied, 'Let the children be satisfied first. It is not right to take the children's bread and cast it to the dogs."

From the context, it is obvious that the "children" mentioned by Jesus refer to the Jews, while the "dogs" were the gentiles. These "dogs" must be satisfied with scraps from the table.

Now compare this narrow view with a teaching of the much maligned Pharisees (i.e. rabbis). They declare in the Talmud *(Gittin 61a),* "We are obliged to feed the gentile poor in exactly the same manner as we feed the Jewish poor."

We can bring many such contrasts between Jewish and Christian ethics. In every case, the margin seems to be on the side of Judaism. Jesus may have taught many beautiful ideals, but unfortunately, he never seemed to be able to live up to them himself.

Apparently, it was difficult even for "Christ" to be a Christian.

Belief in the Messiah is one of the basic tenets of Judaism.
We believe that the Messiah will yet come, and hopefully
anticipate the Messianic Age. But what sort of person will
the Messiah be? What sort of age will he usher in?

THE REAL MESSIAH
by
ARYEH KAPLAN

What is the future bringing?

There are some pessimists who say that mankind is
approaching its end. They predict that we will either pollute
ourselves off the face of this planet or overpopulate to the
barest marginal existence. Others see man doing the job
more quickly, bringing his civilization crashing down on his
head in a nuclear war.

On the other hand, there are optimists who predict a
utopian future for mankind. They see unlimited energy being generated by thermo-nuclear furnaces, the conquest of
man's most dread diseases, and the solution of all our social
problems, leading to a world beyond our fondest present
dreams.

Never before has mankind been faced with such a wide
range of possibilities. Never before has it had such tremendous power at its disposal, to use for good or evil.

We live in an accelerated age. A man of 2000 years ago would not find the world of two hundred years ago very different. But the man of two hundred years ago, if transported to today's society, would find himself in a world beyond his wildest imagination.

He would find himself in a world where reaching for the moon is not a metaphor for the impossible, but a well financed government project; where atoms are smashed and the secrets of life are being exposed; where the dread plagues that decimated entire civilizations no longer exist; where man communicates instantaneously with all parts of the world, and flies in hours to the most distant lands; where beasts of burden are virtually a thing of the past, and man is waited upon by a host of electrical servants.

We need not belabor the point, but the past hundred years or so have brought about an increase in knowledge unsurpassed in all human history. Whether we use it wisely or not, these accomplishments are truly amazing.

What does it all mean?

Why is all this happening now? In all the thousands of years of human civilization, there were many great men of genius. Why could they not bring about the revolution of knowledge that we are now experiencing? Why did it have to wait until this century?

And what is it all leading to?

And in the midst of this, why do we suddenly find a generation that will no longer tolerate war, injustice, inequality, the poisoning of our environment, or any of the other evils that we once felt were inevitable? Why this sudden global change of conscience that seems to be shaking the very roots of our civilization? Why are more and more people coming to the conclusion that the evils of society are not merely the natural consequences of civilization, but are diseases that call for a cure?

Is there any relationship between the information explosion and man's increased awareness of social justice?

We might seek sociological reasons connecting the two. We might dismiss it as mere coincidence. However, there is a third ingredient, one that already affects the entire world, but is uniquely related to us as Jews.

After 2000 years of suffering and prayer, we are once again in control of our ancient homeland.

Again, the relationship between this and the other two could be dismissed as mere coincidence except for one thing.

It has already been foretold.

If one looks with an unprejudiced eye at the world today, he will see that we are living in an age where almost all the Jewish prophecies regarding the prelude to the Messianic Age are coming to pass. Even the most doubtful skeptic cannot help wondering how this could be mere coincidence. The man with clear vision can truly see the hand of G-d at work.

We who believe in G-d know that He controls the final destiny of mankind. Although each individual has free will, G-d guides the general course of history towards His ends.[1] The collective wills of societies are therefore often determined by G-d. Inventions and discoveries come about as a result of the divine will.[2] Governments are guided by G-d to work toward His ends. This is what the scripture means when it says (Prov. 21:1), "The king's heart is in the hand of G-d . . . He turns it wherever He wills."[3]

The ultimate goal of the historic process is the perfection of society. Since everything was created by G-d, all must eventually be perfected.[4] This is even true of man's mundane world, which was created as an arena for our service toward G-d.[5]

This ultimate goal is what we call the Messianic Age. It is the focus of the entire historical process. The coming of the Messiah is a basic belief of Judaism.[6] This yearning and expectation gives Jews great optimism concerning the ultimate future of mankind.

However, if you have ever gone through the many passages in the Bible, the Talmud, the Midrash, and the Zohar that speak of this Messianic Age, you might become somewhat confused. Some traditions seem to contradict others, while the line between prediction and allegory often seems very thin. For many of us, any attempt to find rhyme or reason in these teachings seems fraught with frustration.

One of the basic points of contradiction is whether or not the onset of the Messianic age will come through miracles. Many teachings seem to support the view of the miraculous, such as (Dan. 7:13), "Behold, one like the son of man came with the clouds of heaven." On the other hand, others seem to support a more prosaic view, such as (Zech. 9:9), "Behold, your king comes to you . . . lowly, and riding on a donkey."

The Talmud was aware of this contradiction, and answered it by stating that there are two basic ways that the Messianic age can commence. If we are worthy of miracles, it will indeed be miraculous. If we are not, the Messianic Age will arrive in a natural manner.[7]

Whether or not we are worthy of miracles, G-d will guide the forces of history to eventually bring about the Messianic Age. If, however, we merit miracles, we can bring it about before the historical process has paved the way.[8]

Miracles are not something to be taken lightly. Man's free will is one of the prime ingredients of creation. If man would lose his free will to act or believe then he obviously could not be held responsible for his actions or beliefs. That responsibility is the vital *human* ingredient of man and it is essential that his free will be at all times preserved.

Witnessing a miracle can destroy one's freedom to believe. Therefore, miracles almost always occur under such circumstances where faith is so strong that they do not affect it at all.[9] In order to merit a miracle, man must have such great faith in G-d that it will in no way be affected by witnessing the miracle.

Although some of our sages tried to bring about the miraculous coming of the Messiah,[10] many were resigned to wait for G-d's own time, when the forces of history would bring about this Age without recourse to miracles. Thus, the *Amorah* Sh'muel taught, "There is no difference between now and the time of the Messiah, except with respect to our servitude."[11] We also find many places where our sages teach us that the redemption will not come all at once, but gradually, in a natural manner.[12]

Of course, many of the traditions that we find regarding the Messianic Age are either allegorical or contingent on factors known only to G-d. Therefore, not all are necessary conditions for the redemption.[13] For this reason, the Messiah can come at any time, totally without warning.[14]

In order for a perfect society to exist, such things as disease will have to be eliminated. Thus, it has been predicted (Isa. 35:5), "The eyes of the blind will be opened, the ears of the deaf shall be unstopped; then shall the lame man leap as a hart, and the tongue of the dumb shall sing."[15]

Similarly, other forms of work will be eliminated in order that man devote himself totally toward his ultimate goal.[16] Many such miracles are predicted, such as grapes as large as hen's eggs, and grains of wheat as big as a fist.[17] As we now know, all this can be possible with a technology not too far removed from that of today. Indeed, when Rabban Gamaliel spoke of these predicted miracles, he stated that they would not involve any change in the laws of nature, but are allusions to a highly advanced technology. Thus, so little labor will be needed to process agricultural products, that clothing and loaves of bread will seem to grow on trees. Similarly, as we learn the secrets of life processes, it will become possible to make trees bear fruit continually.[18]

When we think of the miracles of the Messianic Age as being technological rather than manifest, then we have no trouble understanding traditions that predict such things as space flight[19] and interstellar colonization[20] in the Messianic Age, even according to those who believe that it will not be a time of manifest miracles.

Of course all of this would be mere conjecture and even forced interpretation if it were not for the fact that our present technological revolution has also been predicted, with an approximate date as to its inception.

Almost 2000 years ago, the Zohar[21] predicted, "In the 600th year of the sixth thousand, the gates of wisdom on high and the wellsprings of lower wisdom will be opened. This will prepare the world to enter the seventh thousand, just as a man prepares himself toward sunset on Friday for the Sabbath. It is the same here. And a mnemonic for this is (Gen. 7:11), 'In the 600th year . . . all the foundations of the great deep were split.'"

Here we see a clear prediction that in the Jewish year 5600 (or 1840), the wellsprings of lower wisdom would be opened and there would be a sudden expansion of secular knowledge. Although the year 1840 did not yield any major scientific breakthrough, the date corresponds with almost uncanny accuracy to the onset of our present scientific revolution.

The tradition may have even anticipated the tremendous destructive powers of our modern technology. Thus, we have the teaching of Rabbi Elazar that the Messianic Age will begin in a generation with the power to destroy itself.[22]

If the technological miracles of the Messianic Age will be dramatic, the social revolution will be all the more profound. On an international scale, it will mean the total end of all war, as the prophet Isaiah predicted (Isa. 2:4), "Nation shall not lift up sword against nation, neither shall they practice war any more."[23] According to many commentaries, the allegory (*Ibid.* 11:6), "The wolf shall dwell with the lamb, and the leopard shall lie down with the kid," also refers to the peace and harmony between nations.[24] Rabbi Nachman of Breslov states that man will realize the foolishness of war, just as he has already realized that of pagan idolatry.[25]

On an individual level, the changes will be even greater. When nations "beat their swords into plowshares," the hundreds of billions of dollars now used for war and "defense" will be diverted to the perfection of society. There will be a standard of social justice exemplified by the prophecy (Isa. 62:8), "The L-rd has sworn . . . Surely I will no more give your corn to be food for your enemies, and strangers will not drink your wine for which they have not labored."[26] This is also the spirit of the prophecy (*Ibid.* 61:1), "To bind up the broken hearted, to proclaim liberty to the captives, and untie those who are bound."[27]

Some of the most radical changes will be a result of the nullification of the curse of Adam.[28] The technological revolution will largely eliminate the curse (Gen. 3:19), "With the sweat of your brow you shall eat bread . . ." But this change will be even more far reaching with respect to woman. Many of woman's disadvantages are a result of Eve's curse (*Ibid.* 3:16), "In pain you shall bear children, and you shall desire your man, and he shall rule over you."[29]

Woman's status will change profoundly when this curse is eliminated, and this may well be the meaning of the prophecy (Jer. 31:22), "For G-d will create a new thing, a woman shall court a man."[30]

The rapid changes on both a technological and sociological level will result in a great social upheaval. The cataclysmic changes will result in considerable suffering, often refered to as the *Chevley Moshiach* or Birthpangs of the Messiah.[31] If the Messiah comes with miracles, these may be avoided, but the great changes involved in his coming in a natural manner may make these birthpangs inevitable.[32]

Since in a period of such accelerated change parents and children will grow up in literally different worlds, traditions handed from father to son will be among the major casualties. This will be especially true of the values of religion—in such a rapidly changing world, people will naturally be enamoured with the new and dissatisfied with the old. Thus, our sages teach us that neither parents nor the aged will be respected, the old will have to seek favors from the young, and a man's household will become his enemies. Insolence will increase, people will no longer have respect, and none will offer reproof. Religious studies will be despised and used by nonbelievers to strengthen their cause; the government will become godless, academies places of immorality, and the religious will be denigrated.[33]

Judaism will suffer greatly because of these upheavals. There is a tradition that the Jews will split up into various groups, each laying claim to the truth, making it almost impossible to discern true Judaism from the false. This is the meaning of the prophecy (Isa. 59:15), "truth will fail."[34]

It has also been predicted that many will leave the fold of Judaism completely. This is how our sages interpret the prophecy (Dan. 12:10), "The wicked shall do wickedly, and not understand."[35]

Of course, there will be some Jews who remain true to their traditions. They will realize that they are witnessing the death throes of a degenerate old order and will not be drawn into it. But they will suffer all the more for this, and be dubbed fools for not conforming to the debased ways of the pre-Messianic Age. This is the meaning of the prophecy (Isa. 59:15), "He who departs from evil will be considered a fool."[36]

One of the most important traditions regarding the Messianic Age concerns the ingathering of the diaspora and the resettlement of the Land of Israel. It will begin with a measure of political independence[37], and, according to some, with the permission of the other nations.[38] There are numerous traditions that Jews will begin to return to the Land of Israel as a prelude to the Messiah.[39] There is also a tradition that the land will be cultivated at that time, based on the prophecy (Ezekiel 36:8), "But you mountains of Israel, you shall shoot forth your branches and yield your fruit to My people of Israel, for they are at hand to come."[40] There is also a tradition that the Messiah will reveal himself in the Land of Israel.[41]

There is even evidence that the majority of the Jews will have to return to their homeland before the Messiah comes in a non-miraculous manner. One of our important traditions regarding the advent of the Messiah is that it will mark the return of prophecy.[42] Furthermore, according to many traditions, the Messiah will be preceded by the prophet Elijah,[43] and furthermore, he himself will be a prophet.[44] However, there is a basic teaching that prophecy can only exist in the Land of Israel,[45] and then, only when the majority of Jews live there.[46] Thus, unless we assume that this rule is to be broken, the majority of Jews will have to live in the Land of Israel before the Messianic Age commences.

Another important consideration is the tradition that the *Bais HaMikdash* or Holy Temple will be rebuilt before the onset of the Messianic Age.[47] However, there is also a tradition that Jerusalem cannot be rebuilt before the in-gathering of the diaspora.[48] This would also seem to indicate that Israel will be settled before the Messianic Age. However, it is possible that the Messiah himself will accomplish these things before he is actually recognized for what he is.[49] We will discuss this point later.[50]

Into a world prepared to receive him, the Messiah will then be born.

He will be a mortal human being, born normally of human parents.[51] Tradition states that he will be a direct descendant of King David,[52] and indeed, there are numerous Jewish families today that can claim such lineage.[53]

We all know of leaders who have literally changed the course of history. We have seen, for example, how an evil genius like Hitler literally hypnotized an entire nation, bringing it to do things that normally would be unthinkable in a civilized society. If such power exists for evil, it must certainly exist for good.

Now, imagine a charismatic leader greater than any other in man's history. Imagine a political genius surpassing all others. With the vast communication networks now at our disposal, he could spread his message to the entire world and change the very fabric of our society.

Now imagine that he is a religious Jew, a Tzadik. It may have once seemed far-fetched for a Tzadik to assume a role in world leadership, but the world is becoming increasingly more accustomed to accepting leaders of all races, religions, and ethnic groups. We may soon have reached the stage where it is not far-fetched to picture a Tzadik in such a role.

One possible scenario could involve the Middle East situation. This is a problem that involves all the world powers. Now imagine a Jew, a Tzadik, solving this thorny problem.[54] It would not be inconceivable that such a demonstration of statesmanship and political genius would place him in a position of world leadership. The major powers would listen to such an individual.

Let us go a step further. With peace established in the Land of Israel, he could induce many more Jews to immigrate to Israel. Perhaps he would negotiate with the Russian government to allow all of its Jews to leave. Things might by then have become uncomfortable enough for American Jews to induce them to emigrate as well. Witness the decay of the large cities where the majority of Jews live and work. In such an unassuming manner, the ingathering of the exiles could take place.

The Jewish people have always had a profound respect

for those who assume roles of world leadership. This Tzadik would naturally be a most respected leader in all Jewish circles. He might even make religion respectable.

It is just possible that all Jewish leaders would agree to name him their leader and confer upon him the Mosaic ordination.[55] The chain of this ordination was broken some sixteen hundred years ago[56] and must be renewed before the Sanhedrin, the religious supreme court and legislature of the Jews, can be re-established.[57] If this Tzadik was so ordained by the entire community, he could then re-establish the Sanhedrin. This is a necessary condition for the rebuilding of the Temple, as we find (Isa. 1:26), "And I will restore your judges as at first, and your counsellors as at the beginning, afterward you shall be called the city of righteousness, the faithful city."[58] Such a Sanhedrin would also be able to formally recognize the Messiah.[59]

In his position of leadership, through direct negotiation and perhaps with the concurrence of the world powers,[60] this Tzadik might just be able to regain the Temple Mount for the Jewish people. With a Sanhedrin to iron out the many halachic questions, it might then be possible to rebuild the *Bais HaMikdash,* the Holy Temple.

However, if this is accomplished, we will already have fulfilled the essential part of the Messianic promise.

Thus, the Rambam (Maimonides) writes, "If there arises a ruler from the House of David, who is immersed in Torah and *Mitzvos* like David his ancestor, following both the Written and Oral Law, who leads Israel back to the Torah, strengthening its laws and fighting G-d's battles, then we may assume that he is the Messiah. If he is further successful in rebuilding the Temple on its original site and gathering the dispersed of Israel, then his identity as the Messiah is a certainty."[61]

It is very important to note that these accomplishments are a minimum for our acceptance of an individual as the Messiah. There have been numerous people who have claimed to be the Messiah, but the fact that they did not achieve these minimal goals proved them to be false.

Of course, none of this precludes a miraculous advent of the Messiah or any other scenario. It is a foundation of our faith that the Messianic Age can miraculously begin any day.[62] When Rabbi Yehoshua ben Levi asked Elijah when would the Messiah come, he answered with the verse (Ps. 95:17), "Today—if you hearken to His voice."[63]

As both a genius and Tzadik, the Messiah will see through the sham and hypocrisy of this world. Thus, the prophet foretold (Isa. 11:3), "He will sense the fear of the L-rd, and he shall not judge after the sight of his eyes, nor decide after the hearing of his ears."[64]

As the Messiah's powers develop, so will his fame. The world will begin to recognize his profound wisdom and come to seek his advice. As a Tzadik, he will teach all mankind to live in peace and follow G-d's teachings. Thus the prophet foretold (Isa. 2:2–4):

And it shall come to pass in the end of days
that the mountain of G-d's house
shall be set over all other mountains
and lifted high above the hills

and all nations shall come streaming to it.
And many people shall come and say:
Come let us go up to the mountain of G-d
to the house of the G-d of Jacob
and He (the Messiah) will teach us His ways
and we will walk in His paths.
For out of Zion shall go forth the Torah
and G-d's word from Jerusalem.
And He (the Messiah) will judge between nations
and decide between peoples.
And they shall beat their swords into plowshares
and their spears into pruning hooks;
Nation shall not lift up sword against nation
neither shall they practice war any more.[65]

Although the Messiah will influence and teach all mankind, his main mission will be to bring the Jews back to G-d. Thus, the prophet said (Jos. 3:5), "For the children of Israel shall sit many days without king or prince . . . Afterward shall the children of Israel return and seek the L-rd their G-d and David their king . . . in the end of days." Similarly (Ezek, 37:24), "And My servant David shall be king over them, and they shall all have one shepherd, and they shall also walk in My ordinances and observe My laws."

As society reaches toward perfection and the world becomes increasingly G-dly, men will begin to explore the transcendental more and more. As the prophet said (Isa. 11:9), "For all the earth shall be full of the knowledge of G-d, as the waters cover the sea." More and more people will achieve the mystical union of prophecy, as foretold (Joel 3:1), "And it shall come to pass afterward, that I will pour out My spirit on all flesh, and your sons and your daughters shall prophesy . . ."[66]

Although man will still have free will in the Messianic Age, he will have every inducement to do good and follow G-d's teachings. It will be as if the power of evil were totally annihilated.[67] And as man approaches this loftly level, he will also become worthy of a divine providence not limited by the laws of nature. What is now manifestly miraculous will ultimately become part of the nature of things.[68] This, wedded to man's newly gained powers to bring forth the best that untainted nature has to offer, will bring man to his ultimate destiny, which is the World to Come.[69]

Living on the threshold of the Messianic age as we do should be a most exciting experience for any Jew. Other generations have expected the Messiah's imminent appearance on the basis of the forced interpretation of one or two prophecies, whereas we are living through the entire range of Messianic tradition, often coming to pass with uncanny literalness. If you keep your eyes open, you can almost see every headline bringing us a step closer to this goal.

But as also predicted, it is a time of great challenge. We live in a time of snares and temptations lying in wait for the unwary, drawing them away from the Truth. As one great Rebbe said, "It is very easy to be a Jew, but difficult to *want* to be a true Jew."

But imagine a time during which the Messiah has already come. The truth has been revealed. The entire world recognizes what Judaism really is, and the Torah is acknowledged as G-d's true teaching to the world. Those who have followed G-d's way are now the teachers and leaders of a generation desperately trying to make up for lives wasted on vanity and foolishness.

There are two groups. Those who have lived by the truth of Torah, and those who have not, now desperately wishing to become a part of it.

To which group will you belong?

NOTES

1. Cf. *Yad, Tshuvah* 6:5; *Moreh Nevuchim* 2:48.
2. *Sichos HaRan* No. 5.
3. See *Ralbag, Metzudos David, Malbim ad loc., Yalkut* 2:959. Cf. *Berachos* 55a Rashi *ad loc.,* "*Terichim,*" *Yalkut* 1:860, 2:306; *Emunos VeDeyos* 4:7 end; Maharatz Chayos, *Megillah* 11a; *Radak* on Jer. 10:23.
4. Rabbi Moshe Chaim Lutzatto, *KaLaCh Pischey Chochmah* No. 2.
5. *Idem, Derech HaShem* 2:1:1.
6. 13 Principles of Faith No. 12; *Ikkarim* 4:42.
7. *Sanhedrin* 98a, *Or HaChaim* on Num. 24:17.
8. *Pesachim* 54b, *Emunos VeDeyos* 8:2.
9. *Menoras HaMaor* 3:end (237), quoting *Shaar HaShamayim; Tosefos Yom Tov* on *Avodah Zarah* 4:7. Cf. *Barachos* 20a.
10. Cf. *Baba Metzia* 85b.
11. *Sanhedrin* 99a, *Shabbos* 63a, Maharsha, Rashash ad loc., *Yad, Tshuvah* 9:2, *Melachim* 11:3. See *Kesef Mishneh, Lechem Mishneh, Tshuvah* 8:7. Also see Abarbanel, *Yeshuos Meshicho* (Koenigsberg, 5621) 3:7 (56b); Maharal, *Netzach Yisroel* 50.
12. *Yerushalmi, Berachos* 1:1, *Yoma* 3:2; *Shir HaShirim Rabbah* 6:16, *Etz Yosef ad loc., Midrash Tehillim* 18, *Zohar* 1:170a. Also see *Shnei Luchos HaBris* (Jerusalem 5720), *Bais David,* 1:37b; Rabbi Tzvi Hirsh Kalisher, *Derishas Tzion* (Jerusalem, 5724)) 1:1. p. 88.
13. *Yad, Melachim* 11:3, 12:2.
14. Rav Zeral, *Sanhedrin* 97a. Cf. *Tosefos, Eruvin* 43b "*VeAssur,*" *Emunos VeDeyos* 8:6.
15. *Berashis Rabbah* 95:1; *Tanchuma, Metzora* 2, *Zohar* 2:82b.
16. *Sifri* (315) on Deut. 32:12.
17. *Kesubos* 111b.
18. *Shabbos* 30b, according to interpretation of Rambam on *Sanhedrin* 10:1. Cf. *Yerushalmi, Shekalim* 6:2.
19. *Zohar* 1:12b on Isa. 40:31. Cf. *Sanhedrin* 92b.
20. *Tikuney Zohar* 14b, on Cant. 6:8. See my article on "On Extraterrestrial Life," in the Cheshvan 5733 issue of *Intercom*.

21. *Zohar* 1:117a.
22. *Pesikta Rabosi*, end of No. 1. Cf. *Shir HaShirim Rabbah* 2:29.
23. *Shabbos* 63a, *Emunos VeDeyos* 8:8; Ramban, *Milchamos HaShem* No. 49.
24. *Radak ad loc.*, *Yad, Melachim* 12:1.
25. *Sichos Moharan, Avodas HaShem* No. 99.
26. *Emunos VeDeyos Ibid.* Cf. *VaYikra Rabbah* 25:8.
27. Cf. *Malbim ad loc.* See also *Yad, Melachim* 12:5.
28. *Milchamos HaShem* No. 45. *Berashis Rabbah* 20:10, from Isa. 65:25. See also *Berashis Rabbah* 12:15, *Yeshuos Meshicho* 3:6 (55b), Rabbi Meir Ibn Gabbai, *Avodas HaKodesh* 2:38.
29. Cf. *Gur Aryeh* (Maharal) *ad loc.*
30. Or "a woman shall turn into a man." See Rashi *ad loc.*, *Midrash Tehillim* 73:4, *Zohar* 1:257a. Also see *Midrash Tehillim* 146:6, *Yeshuos Meshicho* 4:3 (70a).
31. *Netzach Yisroel* No. 36. Cf. *Sanhedrin* 98b.
32. Cf. *Emunos VeDeyos* 8:6.
33. *Sotah* 49b, *Sanhedrin* 97a, *Derech Eretz Zuta*, 10, *Shir HaShirim Rabbah* 2:29, *Pirkey Rabbi Eliezer* 32, *Zohar* 3:67b, 125b.
34. Or "truth shall be divided into flocks." *Sanhedrin* 97a.
35. Rambam, *Igeres Taimon* (Jerusalem, 5721) p. 5; *Sichos HaRan* 35. Cf. *Zohar* 3:124b, 153a.
36. *Sanhedrin* 97a.
37. *Ibid.* 98, Maharsha *ad loc. "Ad SheTichla."*
38. *Ramban* on Cant. 8:12, *Radak* on Ps. 146:3; *Derishas Tzion* 1:2 (p. 90). For an alternative interpretation, see *VaYoel Moshe* 1:68.
39. See Midrash quoted in *Shevelei Emunah* 10:1.
40. *Sanhedrin* 98a. However, see *Va Yoel Moshe* 1:66 for another interpretation.
41. Midrash quoted in note 39. Also see *Igeres Taimon* p. 32.
42. *Ibid.* p. 30.
43. Malachi 3:25, *Radak* ad loc.; *Eruvin* 43b, *Eduyos* 8:7, *Targum J.* on Deut. 30:4, *Pirkey Rabbi Eliezer* 43. See *Yad, Melachim* 10:2, *Keresei U'Pleisi*, end of *Bais HaSafak; VaYoel Moshe* 1:52.
44. *Yad, Tshuvah* 9:2.
45. *Mechilta* on Ex. 12:1, *Tanchuma Bo* 5, *Rashi, Radak* on Jonah 1:3, *Zohar* 1:85a, 121a, 2:170b, *Emunos VeDeyos* 3:5 *end, Kuzari*, 2:14, *Ibn Ezra* on Joel 3:1, *Tshuvos Radbaz* 2:842; *Sifri, Ramban, Yalkut* (919) on Deut. 18:15.
46. *Yoma 9b, Kuzari* 2:24 (40a). Also see *Avodas HaKodesh* 4:25.
47. *Yerushalmi, Maaser Sheni* 5:2 (29b), *Tosefos Yom Tov*, Rashash, *Maleches Shlomo, Ibid. Shnei Luchos HaBris, Bais David* 1:37b. Cf. *Megillah* 17b end. In *Yalkut* 2:499, we find that the Messiah will

reveal himself on the Temple roof. See also *VaYoel Moshe* 55f, Rabbi Yehuda Gershoni, *Mishpat HaMelucha* 11:1.

48. *Berachos* 49a, *Yalkut* 2:888 from Ps. 147:2.

49. *Yad, Melachim* 11:4.

50. There is, however, another opinion stating that it is forbidden for the Jews to emegrate en masse before the actual coming of the Messiah. This is based on an oath to that effect, cf. *Kesubos* 111a, *Shir HaShirim Rabbah* 2:18, *VaYoel Moshe* 1:10. This is the opinion of the Satmar Chassidim and others who oppose the resettlement of Israel. However, a complete discussion of this issue is beyond the scope of this article.

51. *Yad, Melachim* 11:3, *Yeshuos Meshicho* No. 3, p. 45 ff., *Lekutey Tshuvos Chasam Sofer* No. 98.

52. Cf. Isa. 11:1.

53. Thus, for example, the Maharal of Prague was able to trace his lineage to the Gaonic line of Rav Ha'ai and Rav Sherira, who in turn traditionally were descendents of King David. There are numerous families that still trace their lineage to the Maharal.

54. *Pirkey Rabbi Eliezer* 29, as quoted in beginning of *Yeshuos Meshicho* (our editions lack the critical part); *Igeres Taimon* p. 34, from Ps. 120:5, cf. *Radak ad loc.*

55. *Rambam* on *Sanhedrin* 1:3; *Yad, Sanhedrin* 4:11. Rabbi Yaakov Berab temporarily restored this ordination in 1538, ordaining several Safed scholars, including Rabbi Yosef Karoh, author of the *Shulchan Aruch*.

56. Cf. *Berashis Rabba* 31:12.

57. *Sanhedrin* 4:4 (37a), *Yad, Sanhedrin* 4:1.

58. Rambam, *loc. cit.* Also see *Megillah* 17b, Rashi *ad loc.* *"VeKeven;"* *Eruvin* 43b, Maharatz Chayos *ad loc.;* Rashash, *Sanhedrin* 13b.

59. Cf. *Tosefta Sanhedrin* 3:2, *Yad, Sanhedrin* 5:1, *Melachim* 1:3.

60. See Midrash quoted in *Bachaya* on Lev. 11:4.

61. *Yad, Melachim* 11:4.

62. *Eruvin* 43a end.

63. *Sanhedrin* 98a.

64. Cf. *Radak ad loc., Sanhedrin* 93b, *Yad Melachim* 11:3.

65. See *Yad, Tshuvah* 9:2.

66. *Radak, Metzudos ad loc., BaMidbar Rabbah* 15:19 end; Rabbi Moshe Chaim Lutzatto, *Likutey Yedios HaEmes, Maamar HaIkkarim* (New York, 5706) p. 230.

67. *Succah* 52a, *Zohar* 1:109a, 128b, 137a, 2:41a, 136a, 3:54a.

68. *Sh'nei Luchos HaBris, Bais David,* 1:32a; *Yeshuos Meshicho* 3:7 (p. 56b).

69. *Avodas HaKodesh* 2:38, *Netzach Yisroel* 50.

MY WAY BACK—
A GIRL'S STORY

Let me begin by saying that I had always been turned off by Judaism as a child. I didn't come from a religious family, and whatever I learned in Hebrew School didn't have anything to do with the real world. In general, I got the impression that everyone was merely going through the motions, but that no one was really interested in Judaism. Even my Hebrew teachers did not seem to be convinced of what they were teaching.

Most of the Jewish girls in my school went out with non-Jewish boys, and I was no exception. These boys seemed a lot nicer, and besides, most of the Jewish boys were too busy taking out gentile girls. I was no different than most of my friends, and by the time I was sixteen, I had experienced everything—and I do mean everything.

Even though my parents weren't religious, they tried to shove Judaism down my throat. They got very up tight when I went out with gentile boys, but they could never really give me a good reason. All they could do was hassle me. They didn't like the way I dressed, and blew up when I stayed out all night.

Then one day something happened that changed my life. I met a boy by the name of Greg. As soon as I met him, I realized that he was different. Most boys were only interested in one thing, but Greg wasn't. He treated me like a person and understood my problems.

It wasn't long before I found out the reason why he was different. He told me that he was a Christian—that he had discovered Christ.

I thought that Greg was the most fascinating guy that I had ever met. We talked about religion, and for the first time in my life, it made sense. He told me about G-d and sin, and how one can reach G-d by believing in Christ. He spoke about religion in a very different manner than my rabbi and teachers had. This was the first time that I had ever heard anyone talk like that, and it really turned me on.

I spent many long nights talking to Greg. It seemed like a whole new world was opening for me. I wanted to learn more, and Greg introduced me to the "Jews for Jesus." It was my greatest trip ever.

Soon I was busy attending their meetings and handing out literature. They sent me to camp to learn how to organize and convince other Jews. When I went to college the next year, I became one of the organizers of "Jews for Jesus" on my campus. We had around a dozen members, but some forty kids usually came to our meetings.

Then, one day, a Jewish organization on campus had a program directed against us. We learned that two rabbis were supposed to be speaking against us. Several of our top men came down and briefed us on how to respond to these rabbis. They gave us the points that they were likely to bring up, and taught us how to answer them. I knew all the Biblical verses by heart, and was aware of what "false" explanations these rabbis were sure to give.

I'll never forget the day of that program. The other Jewish Christians and myself sat in the front row, ready to "do battle for Christ."

One of the things that surprised me about the two rabbis was that they were both young and with it. They were also very bright. During the question and answer period, I found them demolishing all of our well prepared arguments. All the smooth answers that I had learned didn't seem so smooth any more.

One of the rabbis really put my friend, another "Jew for Jesus," down. The rabbi drew him into a discussion about salvation, and my friend replied that no one could be saved unless he believed in Christ. The rabbi asked if this meant that anyone who did not believe in Christ would go to hell. When my friend answered yes, the rabbi asked, "Does this even include me?" My friend was prepared for this and he boldly answered, "Yes, you too." But the rabbi was not finished. He then threw the punch line: "And how about the six million Jews who died in Nazi concentration camps? Are they in heaven or in hell?"

My friend was taken aback. He mumbled something

about them accepting Christ at the last moment, but I could tell that he was shook. To tell the truth, so was I.

The other rabbi was much more pleasant. He had a smile in his voice, and when he spoke to me, he really made me feel as if he cared for me as a person.

After the program, I sought out this rabbi and tried to continue our argument. He would not argue. He told me that he was tired of debating these Biblical passages, and that most of our Christian "proofs" had been refuted centuries ago. He said that if I was interested in returning to true Judaism, he would spend all the time in the world with me, but that for dusty debates, he had no time. Just before I left, he said something that burned in my mind for the next few weeks. They were words that I have never really forgotten.

He told me "Don't you owe it to three thousand years of Jewish history to learn about your own religion before you try others? Don't you owe it to the millions who gave their lives rather than accept Christianity? Don't you owe it to yourself to try to meet a real turned-on Jew?"

The meeting left me in a state of shock. I couldn't get the rabbi's words out of my mind. What did I owe to our history and our martyrs? He said that he would teach me. I had to speak to him again.

I tried to find out about the rabbi, but no one seemed to know him. Finally, I got up enough courage and asked the boy who had organized the program. His name was Danny, and he was one of the few religious Jewish boys in our school.

Danny explained that the rabbi had just been visiting, and lived in a far away city. I was downcast. I had to speak to someone, and Danny seemed very understanding.

We began to talk, and I found Danny every bit as fascinating as Greg, but in an entirely different way. He told me how he had come from a nonreligious family just like mine, and how he had finally discovered Judaism. I could really respect the way he was religious. He told me how hard it was, and how he had to explain to his friends why he couldn't eat with them or do anything on Friday night and Saturday afternoon. Danny also spoke about G-d, and his words seemed wiser and deeper than anything I had ever heard from my Christian friends.

I found myself caught in the middle. All my best friends were into Jesus, yet I felt that I wanted out. Somehow, the Jesus trip no longer turned me on. I was starting to really feel Jewish and felt myself being pulled closer and closer to it. It wasn't the dry stuff that I had learned in Hebrew School, or the hypocrisy of my parents. What Danny was telling me about was a kind of turned-on Judaism that I never even dreamed existed. I recalled the rabbi's words, "Don't you owe it to yourself to try to meet a real turned-on Jew?"

Finally, I made my decision. I told my Jesus friends that I was leaving them. They told me that the Devil had gotten me, and that I would be damned in hell. All the love that they had talked about no longer seemed to matter. They were trying to frighten me into staying—but they only succeeded in turning me off completely. I had made up my mind and would give Judaism a chance.

I spoke to Danny a great deal, and he tried to explain the true meaning of Judaism to me. He also told me about a youth group that he was active with, and invited me to spend a "Shabbaton" weekend with them.

I went to the Shabbaton, and I must admit that I had never seen anything like it. The whole weekend seemed to be filled with singing and dancing—a real festival of life. Their prayers were full of life and meaning—nothing like the dry services at my Temple.

Just before the Friday night service some rabbi was supposed to be giving a class. I decided to go, and imagine my surprise when I found that it was the same rabbi who had debated me several months earlier. I don't think he recognized me and I was too embarassed to say anything about our previous encounter. But somehow, it made me feel that I had come back.

The class began with a discussion about drugs and getting high. The rabbi said that it was possible to get high from dovening—praying to G-d. I couldn't quite believe that. But then, at the Friday evening prayers, a young boy led the services. He was only around sixteen, but he sang so beautifully that each word seemed to come straight from his heart. It seemed as if he was flying. It wasn't very long before I felt myself flying along with everyone else.

I must say that this Shabbaton was one of the best experiences that I ever had. I learned so much, and felt even more. When I came back to school, I started saying the *Sh'ma* every morning and night. I even began to try to say some blessings before I ate. It wasn't long before I joined the kosher dining club at school, and I even tried to begin to keep Shabbos.

This might sound corny, but I really think that I'm enlightened. I am happier now than I've ever been before. I don't know how to put it exactly, but I really feel that I have found the true way to G-d.